BEYOND THE DIFFERENCE

The Importance of Inclusive Leadership

Grethe van Geffen

BEYOND THE DIFFERENCE

The Importance of Inclusive Leadership

Grethe van Geffen

COMMON GROUND RESEARCH NETWORKS 2018

First published in 2018
as part of the On Diversity Book Imprint
doi: 10.18848/978-1-61229-984-6/CGP (Full Book)

Common Ground Research Networks
2001 South First Street, Suite 202
University of Illinois Research Park
Champaign, IL
61820

Library of Congress Cataloging-in-Publication Data

Names: Geffen, Grethe van, author.
Title: Beyond the difference : the importance of inclusive leadership /
  Grethe van Geffen.
Other titles: Voorbij het verschil. English
Description: Champaign, IL : Common Ground Research Networks, [2018] |
  Includes bibliographical references.
Identifiers: LCCN 2018021928 (print) | LCCN 2018032278 (ebook) | ISBN
  9781612299846 (pdf) | ISBN 9781612299822 (hardback : alk. paper) | ISBN
  9781612299839 (pbk. : alk. paper)
Subjects: LCSH: Leadership.
Classification: LCC HD57.7 (ebook) | LCC HD57.7 .G4313 2018 (print) | DDC
  658.4/092--dc23
LC record available at https://lccn.loc.gov/2018021928

Cover Photo Credit: Phillip Kalantzis-Cope

Table of Contents

Preface

In 2013, a cabaretier with a background in classical ballet won the Dutch version of BBC's Maestro contest, where celebrities perform as a conductor. In a subsequent interview, Lenette van Dongen outlined the views on good conducting behind her success. Two things appear quintessential. First, leadership is not just a feature of the person, but a quality of the relationship between conductor and the others: 'You do not seize the lead, it needs to be granted to you by the musicians. You are not in charge—well, in a sense you are—but it is a collaboration where leadership is bestowed upon you…A particular kind of leadership, which must just fit one's character.' The second key point is that leadership is more than a matter of leadership techniques: at least as crucial is its substantive dimension. A conductor prepares not only by studying the score and identifying points of conduct. She/he must also decide on the kind of performance they wish to pursue, considering 'the history of music, scores and interpretations.' Technique and substance mutually shape each other, and leadership is located exactly at their interface.

It is this kind of leadership that is central to this book. It really differs from the type of leadership that our heroine portrays later, in a performance aptly called 'Flock,' in which she tales up the challenge of educating a puppy. Authoritative dog whisperers' handbooks tell her it is all plain and simple: 'What this world needs is a calm, self-confident leader. It is just a matter of time before walking at her side will be well-trained rescue worker.' Unfortunately, life and the world intervene and the performance has to shift its focus to 'the path of leadership in days of anxiety.'

This takes us to another feature of this book. While it starts with some wicked challenges of our time, it offers an alternative to the anxious responses these often trigger. It shows how right in that context, inclusive leadership is in place and beneficial to all involved: the leader, his/her organization (yes, even in terms of Key Performance Indicators), and society at large. Inclusive leadership is not understood as primarily a moral duty vis-a-vis particular groups, but, first and foremost, as a form of leadership that fits our era and therefore is crucial for success. Underlying that view is the author's long-standing conviction as an expert in diversity management: in fulfilling complex tasks, smart use of a diversity of talents is a major organizational asset, even more so in a diverse society. Such diversity management, in the trail of Harvard business administration scholar R. Roosevelt Thomas, Jr. is not a moral duty, but a matter of management wisdom and professionalism.

Diversity management essentially hinges on inclusion of a range of people in the organization. This book takes up recent scholarly work by researchers like Lynn Shore (San Diego University), who considers inclusion as ensuring both that people may deploy their authenticity and talents and that they are integral part of their firm's or organization's core processes. That implies a need for Van Dongen's winning conductor mode of leadership, rather than that of her puppy trainer. Thus, this work also relates to recent work on the what and how of 'relational leadership' by European and US scholars like Ann Cuncliff and Mary Uhl-Bien.

Whereas this book has been informed by scientific work, it first and foremost is a practical book, in at least three respects. First, it is solidly grounded in a range of experiences in practices, and it reflects the author's reflection on these experiences as they have evolved in dialogue with practitioners. It comprises a wealth of examples of situations demanding inclusive leadership, situations in which that hardly is being realized and examples of successful inclusive leadership.

Beyond the Difference is also a practical book in that, second, it does justice to the complexities and intricacies of practice. Avoiding the traps of too many handbooks, it does not offer standard recipes and one-size-fits-all prescriptions that seem sound and simply to implement until that moment of deception, when practice appears less simple than assumed. Rather, this book shows the dilemma's that leaders may encounter in real life, and demonstrates how apparently straightforward ways out may well appear dead ends. More importantly, it offers a wide variety of creative guidelines, helpful insights and practical hints on how to overcome these dilemmas. The recurrent underlining theme is that the most productive kind of thinking not in terms of group features, attributed to individuals ('duality and exclusion'), but rather in terms of organizational and managerial features ('diversity and inclusion').

Finally, this is a highly practical book as it contains a lot of practical advice to those who seek to be inclusive leaders. Concrete notions are formulated for each of three core activities. How to *give direction* while providing room to authenticity and integrating people into the whole as Lenette van Dongen puts it 'you must shape the sound of the orchestra; how do you want the wind section to sound within the overall structure, how the strings?' Next, what is proper *exemplary behaviour?* After all, 'conducting is not just indicating the tempo,' says Van Dongen, 'but also about inspiring people. It really is very much a layered job.' And last but not least: how may one *organize dealing with diversity through managing critical success factors?* A true leader knows how to leave the work to the team. Citing Van Dongen once more: 'Let one thing be a comfort: the orchestra can do without me. If I properly indicate the tempo, I can trust their talents. It is just terrific if I can make the difference through good interaction.'

Making a difference through enjoying diversity beyond 'the' difference: that is what this book is about.

John Grin
Full Professor, Policy Studies and Systemic Innovation, University of Amsterdam

CHAPTER 1

Inclusive Leadership: What and Why

INCLUSION AND INCLUSIVE LEADERSHIP

In the past few years, these terms have entered in the business world but they are rarely filled in more concretely. This book offers you the tools you need to create an inclusive climate in your organization and to give content and form to inclusive leadership.

The world is becoming more diverse, and that has also become increasingly apparent in organizations. On the one hand, this is because of the individualisation that makes us perceive our own identities much more consciously than before. For example, employees no longer accept to work in organizations that force them into a mold. They expect to work in an environment that is open for their personal identity regardless gender, religion, color of skin, physical possibilities, age, class, education, permanent staff or self-employed professional etcetera. On the other hand, there are truly more differences at work than in the past. Since the seventies of the last century, an unprecedented globalisation has occurred in a high tempo. From a great variety of countries, people migrate for various reasons to other countries where they settle with their children and start to work. Worldwide, from China to Brazil, this lead to significant culture shocks and the Netherlands, homeland of the author, is no exception. 'Our norms and values' are no longer a matter of course. This was well expressed by an employer in Germany confronted with the influx of refugees in German organizations: 'it is tiring because 'they' force 'us' to reflect on ourselves. Before we had all those refugees, there was less necessity for self-reflection.' Neither globalisation nor individualisation are processes that will automatically end up well in organizations. Together with the variety of employees, information and ideas appear that contribute to increasing diversity. Many people find the uncertainties and lack of clarity that come with diversity unpleasant. They long for the times when they were not bothered with differences at work.

In addition, many countries faced years of recession after the financial crisis of 2008. This recession took so long and was so profound that it leads to a redesign of the organizational landscape. Mergers and reorganizations were and still are the order of the day, and they form another reason for the struggle with cultural differences. Every organization, every department has its own culture; the differences, even among professionals in the same discipline, appear when departments merge. Suddenly there are new HR-colleagues who feel the need to solve every conflict with personnel instead of putting their house in order, or legal experts who do not seem to think in solutions and only apply the brakes. How can one cooperate when the new colleagues are so different?

Whether it is individualisation, globalisation or reorganization, leadership in organizations offer little support to the employees who are confronted with all this. Every manager understands that financial or ICT-systems need attention because they do not automatically fit, so organizations put quite some effort in problem solving in these areas. However, there is no investment in the employees themselves, in cooperation or communication. The assumption is that this will go all by itself.. In this neglect of the human factor in organizations, calling them the most important capital is often a form of window-dressing; sky-high costs are hidden: not just for the loss of efficiency, sick leave and turnover or labor conflicts, also because of the underutilization of team qualities and the lack of development of opportunities and possibilities that do exist and might even be essential for the future of the organization.

Can it be done otherwise? Yes, it can: by working on inclusion and inclusive leadership. People who look or are different are included and not excluded: their talent is used as much by and for the organization as the talent of other employees. Employees can be themselves and feel in the meantime part of the whole. Inclusive leadership means working on an organization where this is reality. But it is not only an inward-looking process. Developments in society have an increasing impact on the inside of organizations, and most of all, the developments related to events in or in response to the Middle East. The top management of organizations often finds them hard to live with; besides there is a huge lack of knowledge about the Middle East or the 'Middle East effects.'

The inclusive leader finds a time and energy-consuming job in dealing with issues outside and inside the organization such as racial conflicts, international, continental and national measuring tools for women on boards, the flexibility of employment and new social cohesion questions that come with the Smart City concepts. Before we take a closer look at the key arguments for inclusive leadership, we first recapitulate some main concepts concerning diversity and inclusion.

INCLUSION AS CONCEPT: THE STATE OF AFFAIRS

Until recently, scientific studies about diversity and inclusion were mainly held from the perspective of being different and exclusion. Most involved were social sciences such as psychology, sociology and anthropology. Roosevelt Thomas, Jr., a professor of Harvard Business School and also the first black professor at that university in the nineties of the last century made a business issue out of a problem that was usually considered as social or moral. That formed the starting point to reflect much more on the operation inside organizations themselves and to study inclusive thinking and working. The diversity of employees was considered as a fact by Roosevelt Thomas, as well as the necessity for companies to be able to gain from a diverse pool of talents. This is why not the different social types became the subject of his studies but the way organizations succeed in using talents regardless the social type of employees.

This approach liberates us from the search for the truth of whether men do or do not differ from women or migrants from the 'original' population, until what generation people should be considered as migrants, and many comparable questions that dominate the discussions and even the policies in organizations. It is not the members of social groups and their diversity that need change or improvement but the organization itself. The discussion is not about why a person is transgender, but about the extent to which this transgender person can put talent to work for the benefit of business; and if that is not the case, what the organization has to improve to make the most out of it. The extent to which organizations are capable to involve employees of all social types and produce the best results together can be observed. Even if insiders do not say that, outsiders, such as customers and stakeholders, will.

Incidents can and will always occur, also in today's universities. Inclusive leadership is not about the question whether you prevent incidents but about the question whether you as a leader are really there and you are capable to open up for real talents. Are you the one to build and expand bridges? At Inholland University we are very good in the recognition and development of individual talents and subsequently in our response to incidents. However, the subject of interconnectedness is still in its infancy. To develop that, we are looking for 'new space' that is less determined by rules and bureaucracy. It is important that it fits on all levels, not just the level of activity of the leader. Inholland has made already big steps in this regard during the years, also in communication because giving direction to diversity and inclusion means also to convince and to formulate the right words.

The largest problem of many organizations is the lack of strategic dominance. They tackle issues at tactical level and that is not effective enough. These are really profound changes, I mention some examples:

- Forget the action plans and project plans, let it go. Let affairs grow and develop for a while and then look further. Do you have a project plan that serves your direction or does it serve your control and uncertainty avoidance?

- Keep yourself as a leader in motion, stimulate niches and connect them.

- Play with instruments that you are using now for manageability, like the system for assessment.

Marij Urlings, Director of Domain Education & Innovation, Inholland University of Applied Sciences

---

So, inclusion means to incorporate all types of employees in the organization. The necessity to work on inclusion arises due to the fact that organizations need diversity to survive, just like in nature where diversity strengthens the species and uniformity can cause the extinction of plants and races. This is why diversity and inclusion are often mentioned in one breath, as inextricably linked. The abbreviation D&I (Diversity & Inclusion) is well-established in many organizations and D&I will be used further on in this book concerning the approach of diversity and inclusion as field and leadership theme.

Inclusive Leadership stands for the inclusion of guidance of everybody and the diversity of employees, customers, and stakeholders towards the indicated direction. To get a good grip on this ambition, I elaborate more on the experience of 'everybody' on being included because experience is also about perceptions and thus subjectivity. Both in the land of organizations and in science, inclusion is a recent concept that is not yet unequivocally defined.

The following definition for example strongly relies on the interaction between colleagues:

> The degree to which an employee is accepted and treated as an insider by others in a work system. (Pelled, Ledford, and Mohrman, 1999).

Or this definition that emphasizes more the condition side of labor deployment:

> The removal of obstacles to the full participation and contribution of employees in organizations. (Roberson, 2006).

In the next definition, the accent lies in the personal experience of employees and the efforts made by the organization:

> Inclusion is the extent to which employees believe their organizations engage in efforts to involve all employees in the mission and operation of the organization with respect to their individual talents. (Avery, McKay, Wilson and Volpone, 2008).

One step forward is the following definition because it clearly shows the intended results:

> Inclusion is people of all social identity groups [have] the opportunity to be present, to have their voices heard and appreciated, and to engage in core activities on behalf of the collective. (Wasserman, Gallegos and Ferdman 2008)

Although still roughly, some good tools for the interpretation of the concept of inclusion are given by scientists. Therefore in the next paragraph we explore the Inclusion Framework, a model of six scientists of Tilburg University.

The Inclusion Framework

Clearly, inclusion contains two key elements that do not form two extremes on a scale but are intertwined like some kind of yin and yang. On the one side, you see the individual, the autonomy and the distinction. The unique character and talents of the individual fully develop. On the other side, there is involvement, acceptance, and appreciation. Central is belonging and contributing to the whole. The Inclusion Framework shows how that works out in daily practice.

Inclusion Framework	Low Belongingness	High Belongingness
Low Value in Uniqueness	Exclusion Individual is not treated as an organizational insider with unique value in the work group but there are other employees or groups who are insiders.	Assimilation Individual is treated as an insider in the work group when they conform to organizational/ dominant culture norms and downplay uniqueness.
High Value in Uniqueness	Differentiation Individual is not treated as an organizational insider in the workgroup but their unique characteristics are seen as valuable and required for group/ organization success.	Inclusion Individual is treated as an insider and also allowed/encouraged to retain uniqueness within the work group.

L.M. Shore, A.E. Randel, B.G. Chung, M.A. Dean, K.H. Ehrhart, G. Singh, 2010.

This model has four variants:

1. When there is little room for uniqueness and little experience of belonging, there is exclusion.

   - This is the situation in which employees who are a 'different' social type largely underperforms or leaves the organization. For example, the huge turnover among female and migrant employees in accountancy and law firms because the evaluation and promotion is decided through a system of partnership. It is not just working like the partner; also looking like the partner forms an important part of the organizational culture while in the meantime, few actual partners in the firms are female or migrant themselves.

2. When an employee can belong on condition of adaptation, there is assimilation.

   - This situation is often found at local and national government organizations. Working at the government offers status and security with employment conditions often better than average. Employees can be inclined to give up individuality at that price. Frequently the underperformance that comes with it is preferred by these organizations over the 'tricky' aspects of handling diversity.

3. When there is a lot of room for uniqueness and the engagement of individual qualities, but the employee involved does not participate in the core of the organizational activities, there is differentiation.

    - This often occurs in organizations who have to innovate but do not dare to make the necessary steps. As D&I officers, they appoint a colleague who is woman or has a migrant background or both in any case someone who is seen as member of the 'target group.' However, in the core activities of the organization employees of this social type are hardly found. This is comparable with other innovation processes, think of the way organizations dealt or deal with hackers, environmental activists and the like.

4. When the employee can participate in the core activities of the organization, including the engagement of individuality and unique qualities, there is inclusion.

    - Well-known examples of people who have achieved this individually are Neelie Kroes or Christine Lagarde. Special talents and strength are needed to achieve this as an individual. Organizations with a good inclusive climate are still rare but many are working on improvement. International companies like Sodexo, Accenture, Unilever, and PWC consider D&I as a top priority for future performance and communicate actively about their inclusive measures to attract a diversity of new employees worldwide.

The creators of the Inclusion Framework stress that balance is needed to handle the two elements of uniqueness and belongingness. Organizations that focus strongly on uniqueness have to deal with lack of cooperation, group thinking, silo mentality, and an abundance of stereotypes. However, with too strong a focus on belonging, organizations risk to suppress certain backgrounds, experiences and opinions. So both elements need to be part of your D&I approach.

> Bureaucracy hinders inclusion because of the playing field of interests. In bureaucratic organizations 'politics with a small p' rules and usually leads to an exclusive culture. Bureaucracy is impersonal; it deals with functions and not with human beings. But that is only theory, in practice it doesn't work because human beings and their interests do exist. Inclusive leadership means creating an environment where persons are willing to step aside for another person to get things done. Nonetheless if someone fights for his or her position, defends interests and covers information, it is impossible to break through that. The most important condition for inclusion is to be vulnerable. And the challenge is, how to provide the right input to challenge also your own group. That is difficult in a bureaucracy.
>
> Mohamed Aadroun, teacher business administration Amsterdam University of Applied Sciences

The Inclusion Framework and Inclusive Leadership

What does this all mean for the inclusive leader? To engage all in the indicated direction demands an approach where participation is built into the core activities of the organization. The creators of the Inclusion Framework specify some concrete practices in this regard:

- Everybody has the status of insider and a voice

- Information is shared

- There is participation in the most important decision-making processes for the organization

This is a good guideline for the inclusive leader in the how of giving direction. However, also the creators of the Inclusion Framework remark that this does not yet provide certainty. The assumption is that these practices support employees to feel and perceive belongingness. Still, it happens that leaders think everyone has a voice and information is sufficiently shared, while others claim that they do not have a voice and that information is withheld. The subjective, psychological side of this still needs further research, the creators state. So that is as far as the inclusive leader can go with actual science. And although knowledge is still limited, it is possible to make a simple analysis of your organization in the light of the practices mentioned above; that will undoubtedly give already some good insights about the inclusion status. Surely, experience teaches us that most employees, leaders, managers, professionals, or operational staff can easily write on the back side of a beer mat who are the ones with the status of insider and who have a voice.

As CEO, you have carried out a reorganization at the headquarters of a large chain of stores that show a reasonable performance. In fact, in comparison to other chains of stores you are doing quite well, but in the light of shareholder and investor expectations, the performance is not good enough. Innovation features high on your list of priorities. Together with some strategic colleagues, you closely follow what happens with successful chains of stores in other countries: what works and what doesn't? This alertness in combination with fantastic ideas of employees and beautiful designs makes that your chain of stores has survived so far but all need to shift up a gear.

The company has worked consciously during years on diversity in age, gender, LGBT (Lesbian, Gay, Bisexual, and Transgender) and nowadays also more and more on diversity through a multidisciplinary approach. The lonely genius designer of the past probably doesn't exist anymore. All disciplines have to consider the production lines, from raw materials to store design and marketing right from the start. By increasing the diversity of insights and viewpoints the company is expected to become more creative and innovative. In a certain way, this seems to work, but you see more mutual irritations than before. The employee satisfaction survey has shown lower results in the past two years without a clear cause. There is more grumbling at the coffee machine and a number of managers complain that productivity declines, although it is not quite clear how they measure that.

In this company, employees can develop great things. Now that the work became interdisciplinary, employees have and use the possibility to switch to different teams. Nobody has a private project anymore; employees give added value to the ensemble but it is no longer 'theirs only.' The possibilities for education are also great. The company invests a lot in coaching of women to the top and in young employees with a migrant background. There is also participation in a project to offer jobs for refugees, a project that some employees are very enthusiast about because they really want to help.

Nevertheless, in a personnel meeting, you are suddenly confronted with a lot of anger. The shared ambition is creativity and innovation. The barrier is that the company needs differences for the purpose of creativity on the one side, while on the other side, employees have a feeling of loss: many things have changed already and these are things they cannot easily talk about. How do you express that you were having a much better cooperation in the past and that meetings were easier? Traditionally the focus for D&I in your chain of stores was on minorities, whether they were women, of color, migrant, young, old or whatever. After the personnel meeting, you understand that change is needed because nobody seems to feel like an insider any more. Employees who are women or have a migrant background only seem to succeed due to the special attention and investment the company has for their 'social type.' And other employees now also start to feel like a minority in their own company: even though they worked so long and hard, they seem to lose the insider status because they are less in number of their social type now and because they have lost their 'private projects.'

A clear direction, in this case creativity and innovation, ensures the common goal that provides a high degree of belongingness for all your employees. Without that the differences between employees at work can easily lead to uncertainties, sick leave and conflicts. The common ground makes the acceptances of differences easier, in fact, these differences will be perceived as an opportunity and inserted for the common challenge instead as a threaten with all the problems in cooperation that come with that. In the chain of stores, the potential is there, but it does not come all by itself. Thanks to the Inclusion Framework, you can determine what the problem is and what direction to follow: the policies have focused too much on the indeed valuable uniqueness of the employees. The focus on belongingness needs expansion and you can arrange for that.

I deal with the what and how to address this task in chapter 5, titled Organize: Managing Critical Success Factors. This forms the third aspect of inclusive leadership.

> The Royal Netherlands Marechaussee aims for both a high level of belongingness and the space to be unique. Our motto is 'making the difference': the added value for society is very important and is shared in daily reality by our people. That is however in the same time our pitfall and maybe weakness. Organizations like ours can be inclined to behave also a bit unique, so it is necessary to verify continuously whether we are still in connection with society. Comparatively the Marechaussee is well on its way with inclusion compared to other arms of the Dutch military.
> Our earlier program 'Courageous Leadership' with values like respect, attention, passion and pleasure has worked out well for internal dialogue. This also effects how people work in the operation. Based on their office they have discretionary power with regard to their actions and thus also in discussions. So, there is contradiction, which would not be accepted in other arms of the military.
>
> André Peperkoorn, deputy commander Royal Netherlands Marechaussee

A final remark: Every leader who reflects on the above-mentioned practices of the Inclusion Framework (everybody has the status of insider and a voice, information is shared, there is participation in the most important decision-making processes of the organization), recognizes the dilemmas that D&I undoubtedly bring. In case of the chain of stores, if you had asked the existing employees years ago how they felt about the policy for women and people with a migrant background before starting it, do you think that policy would have existed at all? And if everybody had been allowed to participate in the decision about multidisciplinary teams, would you have succeeded to create them and also in the tempo that you as a leader thought was necessary? I have stated already several times in this book: diversity feels less attractive than uniformity. Who is going to buy new shoes when the old ones are well run-in and fit so much better?

You cannot achieve a lot without commitment. The example of the chain of stores shows that ignoring signals leads sooner or later to a downward spiral. To work in the spirit of the Inclusion Framework means that with every step you make, you think in terms of process: not just about the policy to develop, but also how and to what extent you can let employees participate and even decide. Indeed, this goes for most decision-making processes; nevertheless, it matters more for D&I because of the specific sensitivities in this field.

An additional factor that must not be underestimated is your own conviction or opinion. Precisely in the field of D&I, dilemmas often occur. When asked whether or not the company should start to work in an open office park setting, colleagues might argue and when asked whether to work with Microsoft or Apple probably even more, but few discussions become so personal and get so easily out of hand as discussions about D&I. Know yourself and be conscious about your own conviction or opinion. It can be a matter of principle. Can you live with the outcome of a decision-making process different from your principle? Define how and to what extent you take your personal conviction into account or find the right middle course. For the inclusive leader, giving direction also means handling the difficult balance between the engagement of employees and a truthful and authentic guidance of the way.

Four Key Arguments for Inclusive Leadership

Inclusive leadership is certainly not an easy task. Employees will not applaud for you nor will the world outside until it appears to be successful. On the road to success, there is resistance because the employees do not like differences and prefer to ignore the pressure from outside rather than to deal with it. 'Business as usual' is a deep wish in the country of organizations, but it is a wish that cannot be fulfilled in the fast, changing world of today. Also, for the outside world, inclusive leadership is a complicated issue, as outsiders ask for immediate change in the organization; from inclusion in education to ending discrimination in the labor market and bringing women in the top of organizations, there is hardly time to reflect and enter in a thorough dialogue with the parties involved. In heated debates, the outside world demands action *now*. Therefore, as an inclusive leader, be prepared for your task. This book provides you with the necessary tools. But before that, I address the four key arguments why inclusive leadership is not just desired but also urgent.

1. Inclusion has real and quantifiable financial impacts.

2. The new, complex social reality requires another type of leadership.

3. Talents allow less and less to be limited by the boundaries of our organizations.

4. The digitalising future does not bring a high quality of life without inclusion.

Key Argument 1: Inclusion has Real and Quantifiable Financial Impacts

It is not the least influential person in the country of organizations who forcefully states this argument: Larry Fink of BlackRock, the world's largest asset manager with

4.6 trillion dollars, has sent a letter to all CEOs worldwide in February 2016 from which the following quote was taken:

> Generating sustainable returns over time requires a sharper focus not only on governance, but also on environmental and social factors facing companies today. These issues offer both risks and opportunities, but for too long, companies have not considered them core to their business even when the world's political leaders are increasingly focused on them, as demonstrated by the Paris Climate Accord. Over the long-term, environmental, social and governance (ESG) issues ranging from climate change to diversity to board effectiveness have real and quantifiable financial impacts. At companies where ESG issues are handled well, they are often a signal of operational excellence.[1]

The short-term thinking of companies and politics in Europe and the USA threatens good corporate behavior and long-term growth, Fink says. He finds it essential that every organization develops a vision on ecological and social and governance issues (ESG) and calls this even a proof of operational excellence.

When the CEOs take Larry Fink's words seriously, D&I will become more and more part of the core processes of companies. The past decades have continuously shown that the implementation of D&I in organization is challenging. Compensation in organisations considers the short-term results but the results of D&I actions are merely seen in the long term. Therefor implementing D&I has not been a rewarding task for managers. Diversity unfriendliness may certainly be a problem but more important is the awareness Larry Fink tries to raise: that we are dealing with an overall transition where we have to go from short-term thinking to long-term thinking and that D&I is inextricably linked to growth and operational excellence in the long term.

---

[1] http://uk.businessinsider.com/blackrock-ceo-larry-fink-letter-to-sp-500-ceos-2016-2?r=US&IR=T

> How was it possible for you to develop into an inclusive, international entrepreneur?
>
> My background is an extra asset; from a very young age on I have learned to switch between cultures and to form bridges. It is a competence or even an unfair advantage, a part of my DNA. I note that it is more normal for me to explore the culture beforehand: what is that Japanese culture? And I respond more easily through improvisation when something unexpected happens, as one cannot learn everything beforehand. In Shanghai, we have a young partner who does not speak English, so everything is done with an interpreter. Last year we were in a restaurant in a private room, in China that symbolizes status and extra respect. In the western world, we would rather consider this as cold and unfriendly. The interpreter came half an hour late and there we were. We did not wait and just started our conversation with hand signals and facial expression; we had a lot of fun together. Most probably they were laughing at us and us at them but we did understand each other and the ice was broken instantly. When the interpreter entered, it became immediately formal again, there was no more laughing, actually that was a pity.
>   Indeed, the Chinese culture is closer to the Turkish culture than the Dutch culture so it is easier for me to understand the facial expressions. I used to think that my competences came from my two-fold cultural inheritance but I noticed that also Dutch people with a lot of international experience have them. They have the capacity to switch in the right moment in international business. Because of my work I meet with Dutch business people all over the world and they also have that broader conceptual framework. They ask different questions and they understand what I am doing.
>   Also, my model of acceptance has changed: when I arrive in a new country, I first wait and see; I allow others to take the lead and I re-act instead of always acting myself.
>
> Atilla Aytekin, CEO Orange Games

Survey data about D&I in the top of companies is published on a regular basis. Diversity then mostly means: man, and woman. In a report published in September 2015, Grant Thornton connects this diversity directly to the results of (listed) companies who take D&I seriously, and these results are very positive. It concerns significant financial impact, just like Larry Fink points out.

> Companies with diverse executive boards outperform peers run by all-male boards according to new research from Grant Thornton. The study, which covers listed companies in India, UK and US, estimates the opportunity cost for companies with male-only executive boards (in terms of lower returns on assets) at a staggering US$ 655 billion in 2014.

> The numbers are revealed in Women in business: the value of diversity, a new report from Grant Thornton scrutinizing the financial performance of

companies listed on the S&P 500, CNX 200 and FTSE 350. Although acknowledging the progress made by women at a non-executive level, the report focused on whether diverse executive teams the people involved in day-to-day business operations outperform male-only peers. Analysis of the return on assets ratio (also known as return on investment) showed that, on average, companies with at least one female executive board member outperformed those with male-only boards in each of the three markets analyzed.

Source: Grant Thornton Global[2]

Grant Thornton states that diversity both concerns the companies' results and societal justice. That is one of the major changes in the last ten years: the surroundings and society interfere much more than before with the way the organization works. People identify with the values they perceive in organizations and brands and then they buy their products or services. Or they feel distance to those values and they do not become a customer unless there is no other choice.

Key Argument 2: The New, Complex Social Reality Requires Another Type of Leadership

D&I brings many advantages for the organization, provided that it is well-managed. I wrote that in my book *Making the Difference* (published in 2010). We are now entering the phase in which inclusive leadership is urgent. When D&I is not well-managed, it becomes part of the public and political domain. No organization wants that to happen, but it inevitably happens when D&I issues in their organization are misjudged. There have been countless examples recently. Politicians started to tweet about it, parliamentarians were asking questions, and managers had to face opinion leaders in public media to answer for issues considered as 'internal affairs.' A selection of instances from a period of just six weeks in the Netherlands, spring 2016:

- *Magazine Folia*, the in-house magazine of the Amsterdam University of Applied Sciences, was removed on occasion of the open day for new students because it showed 'bare breasts,' it led to a much-discussed debate between the director of the university and the editor of the magazine on national television.

- A dress code for female public servants at the city hall counters of Amsterdam led to a real #skirtsgate on Twitter and to questions by politicians.

- Warehouse Hema became national news because its new leaflet had replaced Happy Easter with Happy Spring to keep people

---

[2] http://www.grantthornton.cn/en/Press%20room/2015/News1446101672327.html

(supposedly Muslims) from taking offense; also, politicians mingled into the national discussion about the leaflet.

- The national organization for the housing of asylum seekers did not succeed to provide safety for gay asylum seekers; after heavy political debate, they got a private shelter.

In the same period in Germany and France:

- The Mitteldeutsche Regiobahn in Germany introduced special train coupés for female passengers, with heated reactions of the public as a consequence.

- Air France reopened the flights to Iran and sent a dress code to the female employees. This dress code is not different than it was until 2008, when the flights to Iran by Air France were stopped because of the international boycott. However, this time a storm of protest broke loose and within a day all media and a government secretary were involved.

It is no surprise that the assistance of asylum seekers attracts a lot of public attention. But in case of the other examples, the companies are completely surprised by the sudden public and political attention and they have real miscalculations in the anticipation of internal effects and negative publicity effects. Of course, organizations cannot control the societal discussions all by themselves but these discussions do enter into the organization nowadays and customers ask for appropriate responses.

As said, we live in dynamic times. On the one hand, there are the fast changes, caused by individualisation, globalisation, technological progress, and migration. On the other hand, there is a worldwide field of tension concerning norms and values that does not stop at the doorstep of your organization. The natural consequence is that leadership has more than before a guiding role for the values and norms of the organization, internally and towards the outside world.

> The current KMAR-method is aimed at growth and development: to test things out, to rely on feelings and after that the 'hard' process will follow. That is a completely different approach than traditionally at the Military where the hard process was always leading.
>
> André Peperkoorn, deputy commander Royal Netherlands Marechaussee

Positive examples also exist: companies who are taking the lead, who act in the light of societal discussions and distinguish themselves in their sectors like cleaning company Asito, who is the initiator of the National Integration Dinner and the National Integration Fund in the Netherlands.

10,000 Unique Cleaning Operatives

The strength of color is not just in the skin color but in all aspects that make people unique. The diversity within Asito is large just like it is in society. The strength of color means:

- *Opportunities for each other*

- *Learn from each other*

- *Real attention*

- *Exchange between cultures*

- *Balance in results*

- *Social responsibility*

Asito sees the richness that those differences bring and embraces diversity. Also, Asito realizes that the company forms the entrance to the labor market for many. This is how valuable connections are made between the workforce and our cleaning company, whereby Asito takes on its social responsibility and takes the lead to turn diversity into positive results for every target group. Source: Asito[3]

Asito thrives on the policy pursued. A press release in December 2015 states:

Decision makers in the private sector find Asito the best cleaning company and the third best service provider of the Netherlands. In the yearly survey for the best service providers of the Netherlands by magazine Management Team, the MT100, Asito has shown as the best cleaning company by far. On the list with all service providers of the Netherlands, Asito takes the third place.

This didn't just happen all by itself to Asito. It is the result of years of effort and a conscious approach of inclusion and inclusive leadership.

---

[3] http://www.asito.nl/Over-ons/Kracht-van-Kleur.aspx

Key Argument 3: Talents Allow Less and Less to be Limited by the Boundaries of our Organizations

> *An organization as a box with tasks; a labor market as a box with talents. Recruiters who continuously match the two of them. A world without fixed functions and full of projects. Where the quality of the contact is more important than the type of contract. The way we have structured organizations still determines all too often the way we (have to) work. That changes: the way we (can) work will determine how organizations are structured.*

> – Hugo-Jan Ruts at http://www.zipconomy.nl/2016/02/pwc-lanceert-talent-exchange-matcht-interim-talent-met-projecten/

'The way we have structured organizations still determines all too often the way we (have to) work'—that is so true! This might be one of the biggest obstacles for an inclusive organization. In the past decades, the focus was merely on the way people in the organization deal with diversity and how inclusion could be obtained. The method itself—how we structured organizations—was hardly called into question in the field of D&I; only diversity-unfriendly systems like assessment, evaluation systems, and the like were regularly analyzed. The idea that Hugo-Jan Ruts presents does not contradict this traditional approach but sets a major step forward. He indicates that we are in an enormous transition of the labor market. We come from a world with fixed functions and employment security, and we go to a world where the number of self-employed professionals is increasing. This broader perspective, as shown by Hugo-Jan Ruts, shows that the old times are gone and that we move towards a new type of labor market that will change organizations.

Organizations are stuck in existing modus operandi. The new labor market forces us to change: 'the way we (can) work will determine how organizations are structured.' Many people are fed up with the organizational fuss and hassle. Permanent contracts are given up with a sigh of relief: 'I just want to do my job.' This implies that the actual organizational structures often hamper the reason organizations were created, namely to enable employees to do their job. It is an experience shared by many that the organization itself prevents them from doing the job or undermines the job satisfaction and the feelings of professional autonomy. Lamentations about managers who come up with the wrong instructions or ideas are the order of the day. Recently, I heard a presenter cry out in front of a full room, 'No more managers,' and it was striking to see the great enthusiasm in the response of the public. No remark during the whole congress was received with more applause than this one. People are looking for new, different ways to be able to work, and self-employment is one of the methods to find them. Add to this development that we live in a time of significant transition because of ICT possibilities and solutions and these new, different ways of working can soon become our daily reality.

What is the relation with D&I? On the one side, we see people who feel different, who escape from the constraints of uniformity in organizations and the need to stay within the boundaries of the average through the road of self-employment. After years of adjustment, they can finally be themselves as a self-employed professional. The energy that they lost trying to fulfill the requirements of criteria and systems that were not tailor-made for them and to combat misconceptions of managers about their work can now be devoted uniquely to the quality of the work itself. What a relief! And what an adrenaline rush! Everybody knows already someone who speaks about this with great joy.

On the other side, it is clear that this new economic layout offers opportunities to organizations to become more diverse. This book is full of examples how impenetrable organizations are for people who differ from 'the average' employee. Organizations and the employees within the organization are inclined to clone a certain type of employee or they recruit an employee who is supposed to represent the difference and thus can give an impulse to certain goals, however, soon enough, the new recruit sees himself confronted with pressure to become exactly like the others. The Dutch magazine Management Team in September 2015 proposed that there is a 'war against talent' in organizations instead of a 'war for talent.' 'We try to adjust people all the time to our little boxes instead of adjusting the boxes to the people,' this article says.

> The problem in recruitment for jurisdiction is, in my opinion, that there is no good search for people who are different. We need research to understand basically what is happening. There is no analysis of who initially signs up and why the outcome of the recruitment process is that outcome. Do people with a two-fold cultural background not sign up at all or do they but do they not make it through the selection process? Examine the steps in the selection process: what questions are asked, what atmosphere is created? Is there an inclination to find people who fit within the existing group?
> I know a bi-cultural former court clerk who has very good qualities in my eyes. He went a long way but nonetheless somewhere it goes wrong. What I see certainly for the education of judges is the atmosphere of fear to act different from the pattern in which one was brought up and educated. Students adjust to the culture, if they don't they drop out or they don't even enter. That is the big mistake; it is a world that is too closed in on itself. There is too much focus on how they fit into the group and too little focus on the contribution they can bring.
>
> Willem Korthals Altes, senior judge Court of Amsterdam and chair complaints committee National Police

Self-employed professionals are usually recruited for their strong points and unique qualities. This offers new opportunities in a number of sectors where employees do not succeed in breaking through the persistent system of cloning in permanent functions. For example, most assessments give a lower score to high potentials with a migrant background even those who were born in the country where they are assessed than to other high potentials. Many explanations were offered for this phenomenon during the years, but little has changed. Organizations are stuck in their own systems. And they continue to ask for good assessment results as a precondition to appoint employees even though the disadvantages have been proven. High potentials with a migrant background have to live with this repeated rejection and the feeling to be assessed on the improper grounds or perceptions.

Friend and foe agree that the old ways we trothed during the past decades have shown difficult and rather unmanageable and bring only limited results for D&I. Via the route of self-employment, much more diverse personnel can enter into the organization. Undoubtedly, it also offers other new possibilities such as new approaches for cooperation, meeting and product development. Certainly, this process will not all of a sudden be without problems for the young, the elderly, the workers with an occupational disability, people of color, refugees, and all those who 'differ.' But the road to a more inclusive organization can surely be shortened with many miles through this new economic layout in which 'the way we (can) work will determine how organizations are structured.'

Key Argument 4: The Digitalising Future does not bring a High Quality of Life without Inclusion

The concept Smart Cities is generally interpreted as the development of cities full of technologically innovative solutions. Indeed, almost all initiatives derive from a technological basis and that is, of course, perfectly fine. The new possibilities will drastically change our way of working, caring, learning, living, and moving, and these developments could go much faster than we foresee at this moment. This also goes for the ecological side of the story. Smart Cities offer excellent opportunities to reduce our ecological footprint and live environmentally friendly. Smart Cities promise us sustainable economic growth and a high quality of life. Deloitte defines it as follows:

What do we mean by 'smart cities'?

A city is smart when investments in (i) human and social capital, (ii) traditional infrastructure and (iii) disruptive technologies fuel sustainable economic growth and a high quality of life, with a wise management of natural resources, through participatory governance.

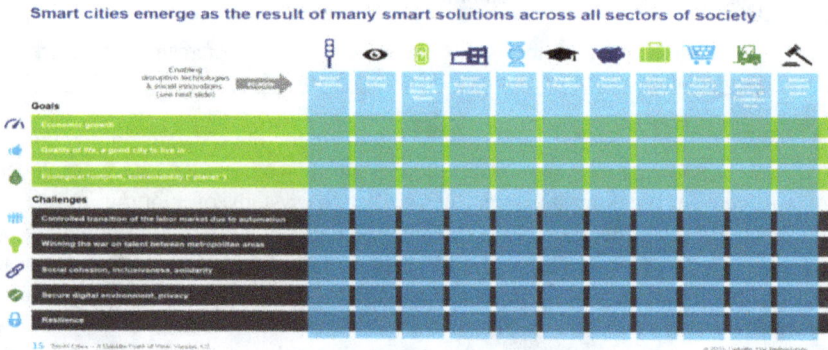

Source: website/publication Deloitte

Where some say that we have just passed through a digital revolution, the consultants of Deloitte claim that this revolution has only just started. Because of the breathtaking pace of ICT developments, a world of possibilities is opening for us and that includes large changes. The model above mentions, among others, social cohesion, inclusiveness, solidarity as some of the five big challenges the Smart City evolution involves. In theory, everybody can profit from the smart solutions but that would not be automatically the case. Indeed, there is the risk that some groups will not use the digital possibilities or not have access to them. Another risk is that groups do use the possibilities but only in order to form closed communities which can mean of course a threat to social cohesion and inclusion. Therefore, Deloitte ascertains that sustainability—as well as social cohesion—is permanently under pressure and that the government cannot achieve solutions on its own. Co-creation between companies and governments is necessary. This obviously implies that companies are able to think in terms of social cohesion and inclusion.

The upcoming digital revolution causes a big shift in types of jobs that this time will also affect the middle class. Predictions say that, for example, brokers, insurers, lawyers, and tax advisers will disappear for 95 percent within the next 15 years because their work can be carried out by artificial intelligence. New job will be generated in the field of data processing and data analysis and most probably in newly emerging sectors we don't even know yet. The majority of the children who are in school now, will be working in a profession that doesn't even exist at the moment. How does such a shift influence a society, especially when this shift takes place within one single generation? A substantial part of the middle class, the traditional connector within society might end up on the sidelines or even in the margins of society. Via which social cohesion can Smart Cities continue to run smoothly like well-oiled machines? It is not unthinkable that gaps occur between the young and the elderly, between the new unemployed and the workers, or between social groups with or without access to the new ICT-solutions. These are just a few scenarios to imagine. The promise of the Smart City as 'a good city to live in' will only be capitalized on when it is not disturbed because the inhabitants of that Smart City batter each other's brains.

A risk that has not been mentioned yet is that the ICT-solutions are generated with too limited a vision because D&I do not form part of it from the very beginning. ICT, just like technique, often reflects existing patterns of thinking and as a result existing models, rules and power structures. Those who design the solutions are possibly not the ones who know how to convert their applications into utilization by a diversity of individuals. Without thorough considerations of D&I the design is useful for people like the ones who developed it and eventually a certain test group. D&I needs to be built into the design from the beginning instead of the old approach that we know from the twentieth century when new products were designed and introduced first; only then there was an analysis for whom it worked or did not appear to work.

The evolution towards Smart Cities demands from governments and companies an integrated approach with D&I as an indispensable part of it. The inside of the organization affects the outside for this matter and vice versa. This is about the way we work, how we produce our diverse solutions and how we let all Smart City inhabitants participate in the solutions; it is about who work for us and the impact of the existing or lacking social cohesion on our organizations. Only that way the promise of high quality of life in the Smart City can be fulfilled. Finally:

> I totally agree that vulnerability is strength. Vulnerability means continuous reflection on your own actions as a leader. Without that there is no connection with what I am doing: educate teachers in such a way that the next generation will enjoy learning at school. Passion, connection and vulnerability go hand in hand.
>
> Marij Urlings, director Domain Education & Innovation, Inholland University of Applied Sciences

Leading D&I is certainly not an easy task but it is urgent and in the meantime challenging and exciting. If you want to be an inclusive leader, you do not need to be bored for a single minute. It is surprising from how many angles resistance can come but also how much energy you unlock at all levels of the organization and outside of it. Along the road of inclusive leadership, your organization will find the answers to a variety of societal and technological developments. This book supports you to shape them and offers a clear framework for your reflections and actions. To do that, first we study a big real-life case and present the Seba Model for Inclusive Leadership.

CHAPTER 2

Toward Inclusive Leadership: A New Model

As shown in the introduction, not only do globalisation, individualization, and the changing labor market force organizations to deal well with D&I; more and more frequently, it is also the dynamics in society and the investors. D&I has become part of a sustainable and convincing performance. Today, inclusive leadership is an indispensable approach and maybe even the most promising approach to give direction and make progress.

Traditionally, we find D&I mainly in tactical and operational personal policies. Focus on the recruitment of certain numbers of women or people of color. Make sure diversity does not pose problems among employees (no news is good news). And try to avoid having the turnover of employees be higher than the influx. Furthermore, D&I is an issue of corporate social responsibility, CSR. We make room for refugees and offer them internships. We also offer places to work for people with limited skills or disabilities. It sounds, of course, like a kind of favor to hire staff which does not really echo equality, but at least it is better than to do nothing at all. We have our own boat to join the Gay Pride in the canals in Amsterdam, and we stimulate company networks for young professionals or even for our wise grey employees.

In the years before the crisis of 2008, the notion of 'business case for diversity' existed. The business case relates D&I to the core business of the organization, be it health care, services, production, or innovation. The business interests and opportunities inherent to D&I are paramount. Policies and measures need to show positive effects for the core business. This is how D&I landed at strategic level, but it was quickly removed from the agenda when many organizations faced a crisis that could wipe them totally off the map; they had to survive first. Organizations that continued developing on the road of D&I were the organizations for which it was unavoidable: the police force for example and health care institutions, as they saw themselves faced with every form of diversity in their daily work; or international organizations for which the revenues of D&I can be found in different domains, such as recruitment, international cooperation, CSR, and the practices of production and innovation. It is indeed in these sectors that the frontrunners of inclusive leadership can be found. Potential problems these organizations face easily find their way to media attention. Surely, everybody knows them and has an opinion about them. It is the paradox of D&I: those who are active in this field hear about their own shortcomings in the news. That is why they rarely talk about themselves as precursor or pioneer. However, despite all the incidents that are extensively covered in the media, that is certainly the case. The knowledge and experience in these organizations cannot be easily met with by other organizations that yet need to start working on D&I.

Inclusive leadership is increasingly needed. Organizations can afford less and less to exclude themselves from the world around them: that world will just march in over their doorstep. Every major conflict we see in the world today had one or more diversity components. A 'diversity neutral' conflict does not exist anymore. With neutral we mean: it is about the allocation of resources, about raw materials, about oil or about gold. Today's conflicts are always also about ethnic groups, about religion, about lower and higher castes, about differences in levels of education, about oppression of women and gays. They are not diversity-neutral; the diversity aspects are part of the conflict and complicate the matter considerably

'DIVERSITY-NEUTRAL' LEADERSHIP NO LONGER EXISTS

This book offers you a range of examples of diversity problems that unwantedly enter into today's organizations. 'Diversity-neutral' solutions no longer seem to exist. The year 2016 started with a forceful example. The newly chosen mayor of Cologne could not have guessed that the months of her election campaign and the start of her office as mayor would be so turbulent. During her election campaign, she was stabbed by a person who disagreed with her (positive) statements about the reception of asylum seekers in Germany. Hardly recovered, she faced an immense crisis in her city when on New Year's Eve, hundreds of women were assaulted and robbed by men of 'foreign' background. Within days, the debate about this event became a fight between the extremes. These extremes can be observed more often in the land of D&I.

On the one side of the spectrum, we find the people who are sure that this is all the asylum seekers' fault and demand tough measures like closing the borders. They do not need investigations and see a confirmation of their prejudices that they communicate loudly and in a compelling way. Moreover, they apply the principle of 'one stands for all,' where the acts of one or more individuals are attributed to a whole group they are supposed to belong to. When one or more individuals are like that, surely, they will all be alike! This is a frightening approach because an individual cannot reasonably defend oneself against the (real or perceived) membership of a group. History has shown us many terrible examples of the consequences of the 'one stands for all' principle.

On the other side of the spectrum, we find the people who prefer to give courses to asylum seekers in order to educate them how 'we' deal with women. They use the assumption that the offenders do not know or understand what they can or cannot do. 'We' know better than that and that is what we will teach 'them.' It sounds sociable and friendly but it totally fails to deal with the fact that there is not even one culture in which groups of men can freely put their hands on the breasts and buttocks of women. Also, robbery is a phenomenon that every culture rejects. In the core, these people implicitly consider their culture as superior as the people on the other side of the spectrum do. Of course, such perpetrators know that they commit criminal offenses! The right question is not whether they do understand it and how we can help them but why they dare to cross evident boundaries and how this could occur so massively.

In between these two extremes was a new mayor on whom all eyes were focused. She was not sufficiently aware of the dynamics she had entered into or, another possibility, she did not have the right advisors around her. Surely a broad variety of organizations must have been involved in the crisis, not just the police or the public prosecutor, also different departments of the local government, health care institutions, and the managing authorities of the train station. Anyway, inclusive leadership means giving a very different press conference than we saw after the New Years' Eve events in Cologne. The advice of the mayor to women how to prevent similar situations sparked outrage in Germany and many other countries: as if the women themselves were guilty of what happened! And beyond that it appeared later that information was withheld from the public; first, there was no question of asylum seekers involved in the offenses, later on there was. At that point, the first leader was dismissed; it was the chief of police who had to step down from office. However, the damage had already been done: all asylum seekers had been put in a bad light with the public and in Germany parties formed opposites who fundamentally disagreed.

With the approach of inclusive leadership, this mayor would first have identified with what dilemmas she was confronted and what ambiguities and uncertainties they included.

Dilemma		
We do not want to put asylum seekers in a bad light with the public.	⟺	We want to be transparent and give information fast.
We are not quite sure yet what happened.	⟺	The citizens are shocked and look for assurance.
We do not want to frighten people and we want to prevent panic.	⟺	We were totally caught by surprised – what if there are really organized gangs of asylum seekers behind this and we have no idea about them?
At this moment we cannot sufficiently protect the women in our city.	⟺	Society expects us to protect the women in our city.
The mayor (in Germany) is not responsible for the police so she does not need to defend them for faults that were made.	⟺	As competent authorities we want to present a united front.
We do not know exactly what happened and why.	⟺	The public want us to inform them about what happened and who the offenders were.
Personal/political dilemma		
I have recently been stabbed by an extremist because of my positive attitude and statements about the reception of asylum seekers.	⟺	I am not sure at the moment but it might be true that many women in my town were assaulted by asylum seekers.

Inclusive leadership is, albeit desirable, not the style of the fast answers. It is a style of research, listening and asking questions. This style is accepted when the underlying values are clearly brought forward from an angle that can be recognized and with occurring dilemmas being mentioned. If only the mayor would have specified that under no circumstances the assault of women would be accepted, a completely different debate would have followed than after the surely well intended advices given to the women such as 'stay away at least at arm's length from unknown men' and 'travel always in groups and beware not to be isolated from them.' This would have prevented the debate to focus on the 'endangered' principle of equality for all people because that debate appeared to be quite harmful. Now the public had an interpretation based on the press conference that the underlying values were old fashioned and unjust, with furious reactions as a consequence.

In this case, transparency also was a value the mayor had to be explicit about. What was her vision on information-supply and how was she going to deal with that? What were the possibilities and limitations? Mention the dilemmas also from the perspective of the audience and they feel a thousand times more understood than when leaders try to do as if they know it all and then moreover withhold information. Here clearly a problem arises with the behavior of the leaders and thus their credibility.

One of the main D&I-issues in Cologne was how such a large group of citizens in apparently organized context could plan for a very threatening action on such a scale, out of the sight of the authorities involved. It raises the question what kind of people work in these organizations: is their personnel sufficiently diverse and familiar with the dynamics of diversity? To what extent do they have antennas in the diverse German world of today, to what extent do they know what is going on and follow what is discussed, in this case on social media? Maybe there are employees who know this and follow it. In that case other questions arise automatically: how come that their knowledge and insights are not utilized? To what extent are those organizations inclusive and can every employee really contribute uniquely within the whole? You will discover more often in this book that D&I seems to be more of an issue 'on the work floor' than at the top. To deal effectively with D&I issues, the top needs to make connection to the work floor in order to benefit from the results D&I can bring. Like I said in the introduction: D&I that is not guided, becomes political. These are organizational matters, hidden under the heated political debate in Germany.

One last remark in this respect. As said, many institutions must have been involved in the Cologne case. All these organizations had leaders and found themselves unexpectedly in the middle of questions about inclusive leadership. It overran them, they were not prepared. The near future demands leaders who have already reflected on D&I and will be prepared when the moment comes. Indeed, this could happen in a large and modern city like Cologne. The mayor of Amsterdam hastened to say that such things will not happen in Amsterdam. Maybe, hopefully, he is right but that is not yet a guarantee for The Hague or Brussels or Paris or London or Birmingham or Zürich or whatever other city. Have a look at your own organization. In case similar serious problems occur in your surroundings, does your organization have a role in it and in what way? Hopefully you are capable to think in terms of values and dilemmas and to make your considerations based on that. Then your advice to your mayor will have more quality than what we saw in Cologne. Hence, you will help to prevent that the whole world is concerned about your town or your organization with all the negative public perceptions and economic damage that come with it.

THE SEBA MODEL FOR INCLUSIVE LEADERSHIP

The example of Cologne shows us that inclusive leadership is not brought about in a transparent world where choices are obvious, on the contrary. What happens inside and outside of the organization seems to be more of a black box of emotions, irrationality and contradictions or in other words: a context of ambiguity, uncertainty, and paradoxes. Inclusive leadership is brought about in the large area of not-knowing. This is how I shaped the model for inclusive leadership:

Seba Inclusive Leadership Model

© copyright Seba cultuurmanagement bv

Leadership does not turn you into the person who knows it all and tells that to the others. Leadership means that you give direction based on values that are shared or that you believe are essential to make progress. So, the term inclusion does not mean that all values are good enough and that all values should be given a place in your organization. The mistake usually made is the attribution of certain values and characteristics to one social group while they are supposed to lack with the other social group. The inclusive leader gives direction and does so convincingly when he combines it with role model behavior. How does the inclusive leader him or herself deal with members of certain social groups, how does he or she talk about them during lunchbreak or at the Friday afternoon drink? Practice what you preach! Also, the inclusive leader makes sure that the organization can deal with diversity at all levels: inclusion is embedded in daily business operations by a conscious management and organization.

For example:

> *Your organization is process and result oriented. This is what made the organization successful until now. For the future, however a much stronger accent on people management is necessary. An internal study made clear that you can strive for growth, higher revenue and more profit, and that you can even have these profit figures without growing if you can reduce the actual labor conflicts and absenteeism. However, that means changing the management style.*

> *Non-inclusive leadership here means: employ more women in the management and attribute 'social skills' to them and hope that this will make the entire company turn into a more people oriented organization. You then*

25

assume that women engender other qualities than men and also that men will not so easily change because of their different nature. Non-inclusive leaders are often the ones who complain that ,women are bitches, especially those at the top of the organization' because their implicit assumption is that women are different from men. The idea that women differ, also from each other, is difficult to grasp for non-inclusive leaders.

Inclusive leadership here means: show on which values the management style should be based and cooperate with you managers to develop and implement it. If your management is predominantly male, you can surely create more dynamics through the recruitment of women. On condition that you know how to lead this process, it will certainly serve the organization. All managers, men and women, need to work on their coaching skills, empathy and communication to develop the new management style together. For existing managers, this means that they have to work at something that was not stimulated or appreciated by the organization for years. For new managers, it can be something that they already bring with them from former work experiences.

Last but not least: are there essential differences between men and women? Yes or no? In my Model for Inclusive Leadership, I refer that question to the black box of Ambiguity, Uncertainty, and Paradoxes. My position is that you do not need the precise answer to be a successful inclusive leader!

As said, the term inclusion stands for the engagement of everybody in the indicated direction. You do not attribute values and characteristics to specific social groups and you treat all employees and customers as individuals. In the example of Cologne, it means that you do not think that all asylum seekers are inclined to assault women but that you do set clear boundaries for asylum seekers (and all others) that do practice assaults.

THE PARADOX OF INCLUSIVE LEADERSHIP

The attribution of characteristics to social groups of people is one of the striking paradoxes in the field of D&I. Of course, people differ from each other: the Dutch from the Spanish, homosexuals from heterosexuals, Muslims from Christians, the high gifted from people with diminished mental capabilities, millennials from baby boomers, engineers from lawyers, etc. Books have been filled with descriptions of the many patterns in which people differ and they are certainly valuable because they teach us to think and work in terms of difference. That increases the chance that people will actually utilize differences at work, provided of course that they have the self-confidence to do so.

> Over the years I have developed into an inclusive leader. Also, I am no longer a co-working foreman. If you want to grow and accelerate, you must dare to let others develop their own leadership. Inspire them, give them direction, do not accentuate the differences but the similarities. Of course, there are differences, especially in the international business world. One can see the patterns; surely individuals can be different but generally speaking the eagerness for entrepreneurship is bigger in the East than in the West. In the East people are so eager they really want to go for it so you'd rather mitigate their speed. On the contrary in the West you'd rather encourage them to go faster. Another difference is that in the West the male is dominant, in the East you'll find a lot more women. In China, at least half of the gaming entrepreneurs are female and also in a country like Turkey there are more female engineers and entrepreneurs. In the West, obviously women have more rights, in the East however they claim them much more even though they do not formally have them.
>
> Atilla Aytekin, CEO Orange Games

At the same time, we know that individual people rarely fit into general group descriptions. Descriptions of 'the Englishman' or 'the Greek' always negate the truth when it comes to a real Englishman or Greek in flesh and blood, and this also goes for all other social groups. This is also part of the black box of Ambiguity, Uncertainty and Paradoxes. The leader who thinks that culture exists knows something. The leader who knows that culture does not exist also knows something. The leader who can handle both points of view as a paradox in every day practices is an inclusive leader. That leader tolerates ambiguity and uncertainty and does not need ultimate truths to give direction and bring the organization further. He or she challenges as well in words as in behavior: all people who share the values of the organization and want to express them belong on the team and will be given the opportunity to work in the core-activities of the organization. Also, if they do not behave according to 'their' social type, what people expect women, gays, Muslims, or people with a handicap to do? Lack of direction often leads to increasing social pressure on the colleagues who are perceived as different, and it leads to the underachievement of those people. The inclusive leader gives sufficient direction in order to make employees put their talents, time and energy to work for the organization.

In the following chapters, I will elaborate more on the three aspects of inclusive leadership:

1. Give direction

2. Role model behavior

3. Managing critical success factors

CHAPTER 3

Give Direction

Seba Inclusive Leadership Model

© copyright Seba cultuurmanagement bv

Giving direction is what distinguishes a leader from a manager. Nevertheless, most D&I-consultants and other specialists in this field hardly consider giving direction as a task for the leader; when it comes to the D&I triangle:

give direction > organize > (show) role model behavior.

First and foremost, they evaluate the personal behavior of the leader. Traditionally, they focus strongly on the (supposed) personal virtue of the leader. The general approach for D&I is moral and even political and much less a business issue to meet with. From the morality point of view, the main issue seems to be whether the leader 'is OK' or 'not OK' and of course, the inclusive leader must be OK, and this is why they focus on his behavior as a role model.

On the other side, leaders allow this to happen all too easily: just do a short training about one's own behavior, admit that it does not always go the right way and then move on again to the business of the day. That is not too big an effort if it satisfies a group of people inside or outside the organization. Just like many colleagues in their organization, quite a few leaders do not yet consider D&I as an integral part of their task and their business.

Of course, behavior is important, but it is not an independent phenomenon. Role model behavior has a good effect in the organization when combined with the other aspects of the D&I-triangle, organizing and giving direction. A lot more is needed from leaders than just role model behavior. More than ever organizations need leaders with ambition, also for D&I. Because all these discussions about 'being OK' or 'not

OK' easily turn into sour talk and rarely lead to the actions required. The improvement of work quality, more creativity, the attraction of new groups of customers or better decision making, those are visible positive effects that D&I can bring for the organization. The morally tinted discussions divert managers from the right path, the path that is just called business and that leads towards concrete results and revenues for profit organizations as well as not-for-profits.

Observation: Showing goodwill is sufficient!?

This week a meeting took place on the subject of diversity in jurisdiction in the Netherlands. It was a bizarre experience, to be honest.

At the start the interested visitor learns that from the societal point of view it is 'of vital importance' to have judges from different cultural backgrounds. Terms as authority, trust, recognition and identification are used to support that statement. Additionally, there is the perspective of the labor market simply because it is already difficult to find candidates interested to work in jurisdiction. This is why efforts were made during years to achieve more diversity. So, the question at stake is: why is it unsuccessful? After a hopeful start of the meeting, that question is rather disappointing. Of course, now the public asks what the results are in the new training group and guess what: on a number of 20 participants, 0 have a different cultural background than originally Dutch. 0! Alas, the leaders of this evening express their regrets all the time, despite the goodwill, it is unsuccessful.

Then a range of reasons is presented why that would be, a list long enough to keep the public busy for hours. Arguments that are proven wrong lead to nothing. Nobody stands up and calls out: come on, we will just do it because it is 'of vital importance.' Gradually the discussion bogs down in impotence. Repeatedly the statement is brought forward that judges are thoroughly trained to be objective and free of prejudice. Most probably that is the biggest problem: the denial that everybody, even judges, are human beings who have bias and perceptions. That in itself is not a problem, as long as you are aware of them, you can ask yourself questions about them and you are willing to correct your bias and perceptions. However, there is nothing to correct if you ignore your own bias.

Then a heavy subject comes up in the meeting: the perspective of young people with a 'different' cultural background, who, this is based on research jurisdiction made themselves, are punished more heavily for the same offense as young people with a Dutch background. To explain more specifically why this is the case, further research will be done. But there is already one explanation: to determine the type and limits of criminal sanctions, judges also consider personal circumstances. For example, if you have a job, the penalty is more likely to be community service because often imprisonment means that people loose, their job. As it happens a coincidence because in society just like in jurisdiction everybody is of good will young people with a different cultural background are more often unemployed than the Dutch (indigenous) young. Consequently, the situation is that with a different cultural background it is more difficult to find a job and because you did not find that job, you will be punished more heavily for the same offense than someone else. I found that a very shocking fact, 'of vital importance.' However, also this fact did not move any leader present in the meeting to stand up and call out: whatever happens, this has to change. Jurisdiction is a very hard, unmerciful world.

When the chairman of the day expresses his final words, he does not notice that he shares another generalization with the public. 'The problem is not in the heads of the people with a different cultural background, it is in the heads of the Dutch indigenous

---

people.' I am stuck in surprise; there were some very useful, even groundbreaking remarks made by Dutch indigenous participants during this meeting. What use is this type of stereotyping? Fortunately, the chair of the day adds his conclusion that everybody present is of good will. When it comes to diversity in jurisdiction, that appears to be 'of vital importance' in jurisdiction: we are unsuccessful but we are OK. Bizarre. When there is a problem in ICT, finances or the organizational structure and years of work have been spent to solve it, would an organization then be satisfied with a result of 0 to 20? Surely not! But when it comes to diversity, it is enough to be of good will, without results. My conclusion: there is every reason for a serious societal crisis concerning authority, trust, recognition and identification in jurisdiction.

As became obvious from the case about Cologne in the last chapter, there are numerous dilemmas, ambiguities and uncertainties when giving direction. They also influence role model behavior and managing, but in giving direction it is first and foremost about the leader alone. He or she can ask for advice but finally stands in person for the choices that have to be made. Leaders are personally held accountable for the outcome: not the consultants and not even the D&I-officer. That is why organizations in the world of D&I strongly benefit from leaders who understand what D&I is about and who can evaluate the painful areas from different perspectives. That role is irreplaceable. There is a tremendous need for guiding leadership concerning the major themes of D&I.

As the government offers less finances for youthcare, we are forced to change our work and base it on the talents and strengths of people. In youthcare that is a major shift as aid workers are used to 'care for' and now they have to 'take care that.' Our ambition and the need for participation lead to an inclusive approach.

In the midst of all changes we should not think in terms of fear and loss, but in terms of abundance. What happens when you think 'there is enough for everybody'? In doing so leadership means thinking from different perspectives: care, finances ánd also power and influence.

Fawzia Nasrullah, CEO youthcare institution Youké

In this chapter, we study giving direction in the complex context of uncertainty, ambiguity and dilemmas. First, I describe four reasons why leadership in giving direction is still less common than required. Then I show the growing dynamics of diversity that characterize our time in a number of concrete examples. Via that road, we find the right approach to address uncertainty, ambiguity, and dilemmas in D&I: the guiding mix.

Four Reasons for Insufficient Leadership in Giving Direction

In practice, this leadership in giving direction lags far behind the need for it. Roughly four reasons can be indicated:

1. Leaders do not know what this is about and 'don't see the problem.'

2. Preference for duality: taboo on dilemmas and uncertainties.

3. Too much resistance: is it really the right thing to do?

4. No responsibility, let alone ambition

I describe all four of them here, because they clearly reflect the context nowadays in which leaders have to practice inclusion.

1. *Leaders do not know what this is about and 'don't see the problem.'*

Strange but true: Even today, D&I seem to be merely considered as a problem of the 'basis' and not the top. While the top of organizations is gathering quietly about strategy and the like, the employees at the basis struggle with real diversity dilemmas: the health care worker, the police(wo)man in the street, the teacher, the desk clerk, the shop assistant, the safety professional, the official behind the counter they have no choice, a world of diversity opens right in front of them every single day. Moreover, it is not just about patients, citizens, customers or suspects, but also about their own colleagues. The diversity of the staff at working level is considerably higher than at the top of organizations.

The leaders of today's organizations are less frequently confronted with diversity. If they do speak to customers, citizens or patients at all, it is usually to the top of the organized associations that represent these customers, citizens or patients. The so-called 'large accounts,' the insurers in health care, the administrative and political top, the business partners, even the boards of multiple patient associations are almost as 'white' as the top of the organizations they are doing business with, and they are also predominantly male and often over the age of forty or even (much) older. These people have not grown up in a world that was very diverse and they are still rarely confronted with it. They 'do not see the problem,' literally and figuratively. There is an increasing recognition of the fact that inclusion is an issue, however when setting priorities, working on D&I usually stays behind, also because it is still unknown ground for the leaders themselves.

> Leaders have an ecosystem of like-minded souls around them. In my case this encompasses merely people who are able to think in multiple frameworks. I hardly see black and white thinking around me. At work this is the same, everybody thinks internationally. My impression is that many leaders in the Netherlands are well capable to reflect on the societal context. It is clear that diversity & inclusion form a subject that is alive; more questions are asked also to me. While asking these questions, leaders are afraid to be misunderstood. The higher people advance in their career, the thinner the interaction between the diverse social groups becomes. There are for example few black people or people with a migrant background at the top. However, there is a clear need to exchange on these matters at the right level, mutually and confidentially. Half of the business conversations I have, tend to deal with societal matters, the rest follows after this exchange.
>
> Atilla Aytekin, CEO Orange Games

Positive exceptions are the socially curious leaders; leaders who belong themselves to a social group less seen in the top level of organizations; leaders with daughters who are blocked by the glass ceiling; leaders who have adopted children that face discrimination; leaders who in former (operational or tactical) functions dealt with a lot of diversity or who worked in international companies where D&I was standard policy; CSR-advocates who think in terms of the P of Planet and Profit and also the People; one or two visionaries who understand the relation D&I has with their business.

2. *Preference for Duality: Taboo on Dilemmas and Uncertainties.*

Dilemmas, uncertainties, paradoxes, ambiguities: those are, at this moment, the main characteristics of the field of D&I. One can find that extremely interesting; for myself, it has always been a great source of inspiration and a continuous reason to observe and research more closely 'how that works.' Nevertheless, today we live in a world where duality meets with larger popularity; they are like this, we are like that, opposites that do not meet and that carry the risk of: good versus bad. Developments such as technology, the recent financial crisis that still has worldwide effects and increasing migration change the world in an enormous tempo. Duality then offers a grip on the world and people do not wish to be deprived of that grip. Duality is also much easier for social media and for the journalistic media, as it is easier to express duality in short one-liners than uncertainties or dilemmas. Moreover, there seems to be a much better hearing with clear opinions that are plain and simple, even though these opinions are one-sided. Indeed, who is looking for uncertainties and dilemmas? Definitely paradoxes and ambiguities are too difficult anyway. At least half of the D&I issues lie in the risky field of not-knowing. Leaders are supposed to give direction but many of them, in a confidential moment of deep honesty, will admit that they simply do not know. Of course, a leader who admits that openly, risks to be considered as weak. That is why duality is preferred in daily practice:

Duality and exclusion	Diversity and inclusion
There is male and female leadership. Our organization needs more female leadership.	There is no male or female leadership. Our organization needs different dynamics in leading teams.
All Syrian refugees behave homophobic and bad against women.	Some Syrian refugees do that, others don't.
Refugees need time to overcome their traumas, learn the language and follow courses, or: all refugees have to enter the labor market as soon as possible.	Research shows us that the old practice of learning the language, following courses and overcoming traumas first has limitations and drawbacks we will work with new, parallel tracks for refugees and a more individual approach.
Mankind consists of gay people and straight people; it is usually clear who is what.	Sexual identity is fluid and often not identifiable and by the way that doesn't matter.
There are a lot more gay men in health care than in logistics because they are more feminine and caring.	In healthcare being gay is more accepted than in logistics, research has shown. That is probably why there are more gays at work in health care than in logistics or, another possibility, in logistics they do not come out.
Engineers are rational, nurses are rather emotional.	Engineers often work in an environment that appeals to ratio, for nurses that is different. But eh, what does the workplace demand? That is what it is about!
A course taught us the characteristics of Turks and Moroccans and how we have to deal with Moroccan and Turkish patients and their families.	A course taught us about our own identity and how we can best deal with the multiple identities of Moroccan and Turkish (and other) patients and their families.
In addition to many healthy employees we also make room for employees with disabilities.	We focus on the strengths of people; our challenge is to evaluate in the best way who can do what and who best fits in where.
We conclude an agreement to help employees with disabilities who are greatly distanced from the labor market.	We want a social agreement that is social for all people with disabilities.
Elderly workers are more expensive, less flexible and less fit; younger workers are cheaper, more flexible and healthier.	We develop an optimized mix to use the talents of younger and elderly workers in the best way and yes, that costs time and efforts but it pays off!
Elderly workers have life experience and can coach younger employees to transfer their experience.	Some elderly workers are able to work as coach, others aren't. There are different ways of learning, not every young employee learns through coaching.

Islamic employees fast during the Ramadan do not eat pork and the women weir a head scarf.	Employees decide about their own identity, religious or not and how they express it.

Speaking in terms of duality guarantees messages will be heard. For a leader, that feels better than to be considered as a softie. Or, like a top official told me ten years ago: 'I do understand you and you are right of course, but it is too complicated for me. I just tell my directors how much women and people of color they should employ and all the rest will follow.' The organization concerned however still waits for 'all that rest to follow.' Indeed, it was a very clear instruction back then even though it did not offer long term results. The directors knew exactly what was expected from them and also what they could resist against; resistance that was largely present. This is how different parties arose, each with their own unwavering certainties, while uncertainty avoidance and an open, investigative way of working are extremely important conditions for successful long term, results in D&I.

> Every year, our Dutch Dream Foundation organizes an entrepreneurial journey to a specific country; this year we went to Romania. When we were talking about next year's destination, I proposed Iran. It is a country with a lot of dynamics and economic opportunities now that the boycott has been ended. Thus, a discussion started, what does this mean for the female entrepreneurs in our group? Because in Iran women are obliged to wear a headscarf. I am inclined to approach this as an instrument, and to leave religion out of it. Comparable with Japan, where you take into account that Japanese bow first and only then eventually shake hands, or that you offer your business card with two hands in China. But well, of course I am not a woman and female entrepreneurs thought differently about it. In such a discussion, I noticed that you have to look for the question behind the question. First it seems to be about the head scarf itself, but further inquiry made a female entrepreneur say, 'ten years ago I would have done it but after the terrorist attacks in Paris I wouldn't do it anymore.' Or it is about certain statements in the media that one has personalized. Such issues demand a great deal of personal attention and as a leader there is often of course a lack of time. I advocate not to leave countries like Iran aside, but to be present there, to maintain a dialogue and do business, also as a woman. It is not isolation but connection that shapes the future.
>
> Atilla Aytekin, CEO Orange Games

3. Too much resistance: is it really the right thing to do?

Have you ever given a course of time management or project management? And a course about D&I? Then you know the difference! Time management and project management feel like a relaxed getaway compared to D&I. All participants naturally start to work. It is rarely necessary to start a discussion about utility and need of the course. The participants like to learn what it is and how to do it. This is a completely different process for D&I. The participants seem to be startled that they ended up in a course like that. Without yet knowing about the content of that day's program, they already point out for what colleagues the D&I course would be more suitable: their manager, for example, or a certain other team in the organization. They ask if there are any D&I policies at all in their organization, if not the course would be useless. They struggle with a heavy workload and in the light of all these other important issues that are at stake, they wonder why the D&I course is a priority right now. And if it has to be done today anyway, can we please finish early at three o'clock? Thank you very much.

With understanding, sense of humor and determination a trainer can go far and the same thing goes for the leader. Admittedly, a leader who chooses D&I as a priority for the organization meets with resistance and gets opposition: more than with other issues. And this leader must be able to explain it very well, otherwise the Supervisory Boards are also unhappy about it. So yes, when giving direction leads to a path where you have to wade through the sucking mud, then you will think twice before you start. Because how important can it really be? It seemed to be so urgent, but at the encounter of so much resistance, surely doubts arise. It is a paradox: D&I asks for priorities to be set but if you as a leader set those priorities, the end result of your D&I-efforts risk to be rather negative than positive. The hope that it will all be sorted out in due course might then win from vision and deliberate actions concerning D&I. There are always other issues that can be taken on with more appreciation and an easier route to success.

> There are no fixed norms or groups or behaviors that are suitable. Up until forty years ago Dutch society maintained a 'pillar' system (a compartmentalised society divided along religious and political lines) that no longer exists now. Along with the increasing diversity in society there are no longer obvious rules. That is difficult to understand and handle. Government organizations however have to understand that and learn how to deal with it.
> It is like in the Provo-movement in the sixties of the twentieth century: suddenly behavior and manners were different. People no longer spoke in a polite way to judges and they just laid their feet at the table. They did not show any respect for authority. In that time, that was quite difficult too. It is worth a lot when judges can react lightly and with humor, like a famous Dutch politician once did when someone in the public called 'asshole' to him and he just answered: 'Thank you for introducing yourself to me, my name is Wiegel.'
>
> Willem Korthals Altes, senior judge Court of Amsterdam and chair complaints committee National Police

4. No responsibility, let alone ambition

Sometimes things go wrong in a way that is clear and visible for everyone. Think of the nominations for Oscars in 2016 where hardly any actor of color was nominated although that would be impossible when related to numbers of actors. Or in a country like the Netherlands where the prime minister states that there is indeed discrimination in the labor market but that it is not possible for him to do something about it; people with a migrant background have to 'penetrate' the networks themselves.

These are two public examples. However, these situations occur in many ways, in small and large forms on a daily basis in all kinds of organizations. All too often organizations recognize that D&I does not come naturally to us. 'Even when people are green and come from Mars, everybody is welcome to work here' and 'I do not discriminate.' It can be observed that colleagues who do see the need of D&I in the organization often colleagues at working level or who experience exclusion themselves start by convincing their peers and managers that it 'really is an issue.' Worst case scenario they become a Miss or Mister Diversity and end up with a burn-out after one or two years. In the best case, there is recognition for their warning. Anyway, the good yields of D&I is far out of reach, even though they would exactly form the motor of a successful approach.

> Recently I was at a meeting of the National Television and Radio broadcasting about diversity and the discussion there had a tune like 'just make it a bit more diverse and it will all change by itself.' This meeting was in fact one other of these box-checking meetings. I heard nothing new, there were some international guests and there was a test to measure prejudices but the most interesting question is: what does the actual leadership at NTR miss that prevents a breakthrough? As national organization, they do not depend on advertising revenues, they are funded with public money and still more conservative than commercial broadcasters. Why is there no leader who walks in the room, looks for great talent and says: OK guys, let's just do it. And the resistance, we will just destroy it. I do not see such a leadership at NTR.
>
> What the commercial broadcaster RTL dares to do with RTL Late Night's Humberto Tan and all the people they bring in is much more progressive than the Dutch national broadcaster. They are so far away from society! It is bizarre that I got used to the idea that what I see and live in the street is never found on national television. To get used to such an idea is in fact quite some conditioning. Real steps are not taken by the public broadcaster. One editor-in-chief just said openly that he does not want a woman with a headscarf because it evokes the wrong associations. And the norm, apparently that does not evoke any associations? The dominant culture creates and protects the standard because it is within the sphere of influence, under control.
>
> Mohamed Aadroun, teacher business administration Amsterdam University of Applied Sciences.

To take responsibility for D&I in the organization means a lot more than just recognizing the facts. D&I is a surprising subject. Compare it for example with the recognition: 'our product has a bad quality' or 'our employees do not have the required skills.' Normally immediate action would be taken. However, D&I has difficulty to find ownership in the organization, due to the combination of ignorance and lack of ambition. When a product has a bad quality or employees lack of the required skills, leaders know what kind of measures they should take and they can act quickly and decisively. But for D&I, they look into the black hole of ambiguity, uncertainty and paradoxes without good knowledge what this is about, what their role is and how to perform it. If they are not ready to be open, investigate and learn, the confrontation with D&I issues will transform into avoidance instead of ambition.

> The capacity to learn actively oneself and to dare is probably more important than expertise because it breaks routines.
>
> Marij Urlings, director Domain Education & Innovation, Inholland University of Applied Sciences.

So far, the four global reasons why, in daily practice, leadership in giving direction lags far behind the need for it. As a consequence, there are relatively few possibilities to pick up tricks from other leaders. Moreover, there is no clear compass.

NEW DYNAMICS IN THE 21ST CENTURY: TOWARD A GUIDING MIX

Giving direction in issues like D&I means working in a dynamic environment where developments can't easily be predicted. A number of these issues already existed in the 20th century, but many situations are also new. Some examples of issues in an ambiguous, uncertain or paradoxal context:

- You manage a hospital or a school that has always celebrated the 5 December (Sinterklaas[4]). But since a few years there are protests against Black Peter because quite some employees and patients or their parents consider this black helper of Sinterklaas as a racist remnant from the Dutch colonial past in slavery. Black Peter is a racist expression, they think and it needs to be abolished. Among employees as well as among your stakeholders however a hard-core group has formed that totally disagrees with this and insists on continuing the December 5th celebrations with Black Peter in its

---

[4] The Netherlands celebrates a specific day, the 5th of December, where all the children and often the grown-ups get presents from Sinterklaas. The celebrations are not only at home, in many organisations children of employees are invited to celebrate at work. Sinterklaas looks quite a lot like Santaclaus that is celebrated in Christmas time in other countries, but there are some varieties. Although Sinterklaas originates from Myra in actual Turkey where he was a bishop, the tradition wants Sinterklaas to come from Spain on a steamboat, riding on a white horse and accompanied by many helpers, Zwarte Pieten, guys with a black skin. They help Sinterklaas to organize the presents, to punish the children that didn"t do good, to spread candies and other nice eatable stuff all over the houses. They climb in and out of chimneys to put presents into the shoes that are placed in front of the chimneys and rumours say this is why they are so black. The yearly discussion in the Netherlands is: is this a racist tradition? Is this about white superiority and black slavery? Is this just a nice tradition that everybody should enjoy, or is this something that should be changed fundamentally? Some parties make Sinterklaas black and Zwarte Piet white, just as a statement. For sure, many expats that meet Sinterklaas and his Zwarte Pieten for the first time are shocked and think it is an unacceptable tradition. They cannot believe that they see this in the Netherlands. However, the tradition stands superstrong; the Dutch resist to any notion of racism in relation to this yearly party. They do not accept the views of outsiders on this event that is as generally celebrated as Santaclaus presents are in many other countries.

original shape. Before December 5th has even arrived, the atmosphere has already been ruined.

- Your organization hardly has any women at the top or subtop. In the Supervisory Board one woman can be counted. The majority of the top means that it will all be sorted out in due course. The majority of the subtop is not convinced about that. The subtop also indicates the national law for governance that wants 30 percent of women in the top of organizations and obliges organizations to comply or explain. Subtoppers want positive action for women, otherwise the 30 percent will never be reached, they state. If that would be true, that means the quality of the candidates is insufficient anyway, is the response of the top.

- You manage a museum of antiquities that produces the most beautiful expositions. One day, you see yourself confronted with a regime change in the specific region of a country that has provided you with many marvelous antiquities for a special exposition your staff worked on for two years. When the exposition is finished, the new regime of the region claims that the antiquities can just be returned to them because they are now the ones responsible for that cultural heritage. But the old regime that just lost that region protests because the claims of the new regimes, as well as their actions, would be illegal. And there you are, with all those beautiful but difficult-to-preserve antiquities, while the next exposition needs to be arranged.

- You have a large ICT company that gets more and more opportunities to work on Smart City solutions. The Smart City of the future surely has a very diverse population. The staff of your ICT company, however, is very different from that diversity, they are mainly white men under the age of forty who produce and develop the solutions. You see clear possibilities for your business in the cooperation with governments but they have expressed some doubts about the match between the solutions that your company offers and the population they are supposed to work for. What guarantees can you give that the solutions will be broadly used?

- Your company has made several acquisitions in the Netherlands and Germany. However hard times follow and the final result of all this is that your company is subject to acquisition by a Turkish consortium. Nobody in your company has a clue about the way Turks do business. Until now, Turks were mainly associated with the cleaners who enter the building after five o'clock in the evening.

- You manage a national museum with a lot of statues and paintings. Naked expressions are part of the collection. The prime minister of a strict Islamic country visits your country in an important trade mission: it is about many billions in contracts to be signed on the spot, very good for your national business. The government proposes to visit your museum and even sign certain contracts there, in front of the unique pieces of arts your museum shows. That would give a major boost to your museum. However, a condition is that you cover all the statues and paintings that show naked forms so that the prime minister does not take any offense to the nudes when he passes. And eh, another detail: you are a woman, so it would be nice if you could wear a beautiful headscarf for the occasion.

- You manage an international music festival that is, year after year, a successful creative and music-oriented event. It has so far been flawless except maybe some accusations about secret cooperation between countries in giving each other mutually high points. But now a country decides to produce a rather political song that addresses a conflict this country has with another country that also participates.

- You acquire an attractive assignment of a company in a Middle Eastern country. But the company asks for a written statement that none of the employees engaged are Jewish. Or they ask not to send anybody to the Middle East who is gay. Or they impose specific requirements on clothing and behavior of female employees.

Giving direction is keeping a keen focus on your goals and the strategy and values of your company; that also applies to business. In a context of ambiguity, uncertainty, and paradoxes, you can only succeed in giving direction when your analysis is crystal clear for people and the core of the direction you want to choose stands on solid foundations. So, you do not say that there is no doubt; you indicate what the doubts are and what is beyond doubt. In doing so, you position the organization at the level of values and in the meantime, you show to what extent progressive insights can offer a suitable and useful resource. I apply this to the examples mentioned above.

The Guiding Mix for Sinterklaas and Black Peter in Amsterdam

A great example of Inclusive Leadership was shown by Aalbersberg, the chief of police in Amsterdam, in the period towards Sinterklaas in 2015. Sinterklaas is celebrated at work in the force while the employees' children are invited as well. Aalbersberg wrote a memo to all employees that could be argued about without end but that is showing a clear direction based on the values of the organization. He states that equality forms the basis of the work of the Amsterdam police force and that this is what he also expects in the Sinterklaas celebrations. Thus, no Black Peter was positioned as a servant of Sinterklaas. Moreover, he refers to the existing policies in D&I and a discrimination-free work environment for all employees. Hence to celebrate with Black Peters only is no longer allowed. Aalbersberg encourages the appearance of multicolored Peters as well as a dialogue about eventual sensitivities and solutions for them. Finally, he reminds all that this is a (children's) party that should rather not be disturbed by discussion during the festivities themselves. There you have it, a clear guiding mix:

- Equality as the basis of the work of the Amsterdam police force.

- A discrimination-free work environment.

- Active dialogue.

- Let the party be the party.

People in the organization can agree or disagree, but at least they get a grip on the matter. Here is not a leader who lets the working force find it out all by themselves or who is afraid of resistance. The message shows an explicit ambition and the chief of police takes personal responsibility for it. If ever any subject formed 'quicksand' during the last years, it was certainly the Black Peter debate in the Netherlands. This chief of police effectively put a board over the mud in 2015 that his employees, happily, under protest or otherwise, could use.

Of course, in the heat of the national Dutch debate about Black Peter this did not pass unseen. A decision of a chief of police in this respect draws major press publicity. 'Black Peter no longer welcome in police stations in Amsterdam,' were the headlines of the Amsterdam newspaper Het Parool in the good tradition of the desire of duality as mentioned above. Indeed, this was not what the memo of the chief of police said, but apparently dual language is understood better by the readers of Het Parool than the more nuanced language of D&I. The journal Metro News did better with the headline 'Black Peter alone not welcome at police' and the Dutch Telegraph simply headed 'Police repels black.' But apart from the loud headlines above the articles in newspapers and on websites, it appeared that journalists could hardly find good arguments against the guiding mix as presented by the chief of police. The message provoked no more than a gust of wind in news land.

The approach of this example is also applicable to the above-mentioned cases of women at the top and the museum of antiquities. The case of women at the top clearly shows that there is a common value: men and women are in this together and it is even desirable when they cooperate also at the top. Difference of opinions exists about the route to achieve that. So at least you have an important starting point in the perception of (a) value for the organization. That offers you the opportunity to give direction. You can build upon that starting point to start further dialogue where you can of course press for concrete results one way or the other. Surely there is a risk that women in the subtop will leave the organization when little progress is made. Headhunters will easily spot them for top positions in other, maybe even competing organizations. This is how you can create a sense of urgency. Thus, you have already some important ingredients for the guiding mix in this case.

The museum of antiquities can build upon the core value of prudent conservations of antiquities. The path the museum can walk probably leads to a judge or the government; in any case, a deliberate path to go is part of the guiding mix. Also in this case much internal debate will have to be met with, especially when there is personal involvement of staff members with one party or the other that claim the ownership of the antiquities. Define the right time and tune for this discussion; it can and should not overshadow the day-to-day work because of a lack in leadership.

The Guiding Mix for Smart City Solutions

The example of the ICT company seems to have a very different nature; nevertheless it can also be approached with the same guiding mix. There are obvious opportunities for your business in cooperation with governmental organizations, but they express their doubts: is there a sufficient match between the solutions offered by your company and the population they are meant to serve? You need a good directive story to tell. Is it possible to personally interview the persons who have expressed their doubts, then do so? It is important to know what exactly their hesitations are. Who are 'the population' for them? Who are the supposed non-users of the offered solutions and why, according to your interlocutors?

After that, be very clear. When you are on the same level about the idea of who 'the population' are, then indicate how you know that the solutions your company offers will be used by all or who will be the early adaptors and where you see possible risks. Determine with your interlocutors what the road will be to reduce the risks for example working with panels with a diversity of users, or changing (increasing the diversity) of your development teams. Another option is to involve your partner, for example a local government, in that responsibility. This is of course related to the nature and the extent of the solution.

Your guiding mix can then be:

- All citizens profit from Smart City solutions.

- *A design for all.*

- We develop together with our clients, and/or we work with development teams that are diverse and inclusive.

- A periodic check with our partners about their perceptions of design for all quality

The approach of this example is also applicable to the above-mentioned case of the Turkish acquisition. Here, too, you find obvious opportunities in cooperation, and you need a good directive story to tell. You already know from earlier experiences with acquisitions in Germany that national or cultural aspects are going to play an important role in the process. A problem is that you and your colleagues on the Board are a lot less familiar with the Turkish business culture than the German one. So, you start by identifying existing knowledge and experience in the organization. You define who can be the forerunners and what the possible risks are. Determine with your interlocutors what the path will be to reduce the risks for example by giving a role to certain employees and encourage others to acquire more knowledge and experience or by involving experts from outside the company. And seek the dialogue with the Turkish company, very successful business people who, just like your organization, only benefit from good cooperation for future success. Your guiding mix is then, for example:

- Cooperation for future success comes first.

- We create a staff department or internal network as knowledge center, helpdesk and sparring partner.

- We are willing to learn and we invest in that.

- We do not talk *about*, but talk *with*.

The Guiding Mix in Case of Inevitable Painful Choices

Three cases have both a political and an international dimension: the case of the national museum, of the international music festival and of the assignment of a company in a Middle Eastern country. They need timely choices because the visit of the prime minister is already planned, the deadlines for the music festival have been set, and the Middle Eastern assignment must be delivered within the foreseeable future. Whatever choices you make as a leader, they have consequences on the level of values and involve heavy debate:

- If you, as director of the national museum, decide to cover nudes in paintings or statues and you yourself wear a headscarf on behalf of the visit of a strict Islamic prime minister, you will meet with a lot of criticism that you deny or even relinquish Western values; if you don't, you have a problem with the government (your main financial sponsor) and you miss an important moment for PR. And do not assume too quickly that in the West, we would never give in to Islamic demands like that; on behalf of the visit of the prime minister of Iran to Rome in 2016, all nudes were neatly covered with a sheet.

- If you, as manager of the international music festival, accept the political submission, that can be the first step to a political international music festival and you do not want that; if you do not accept the submission, you might end up in the impossible discussion about what is political in songs and what isn't. Moreover, one or more countries might withdraw their submissions from the music festival because they do not agree with your decision.

- If you accept the demands of your client in the Middle East, you can expect the same criticism as the director of the national museum because you thwart Western values and even human rights – the only 'advantage' you have is that your decision will not come into public as fast as the museum directors' decision (and a question to ask in this respect is: does that influence your decision making?); if you do not accept the demands, you might as well loose the assignment. You can try to negotiate to find out if things are really as black as they seem, but every compromise will bring you serious problems as well.

As said at the introduction to the Model for Inclusive Leadership, the term *inclusion* does not mean that all values are good enough and deserve their own place in the organization. Inclusion stands for the engagement of everybody in the indicated direction. Nonetheless, in these three cases, the choices to be made can really hurt. Your decision will clearly show which values prevail for you. Moreover, whatever you decide, it will present a risk for your own position, and it is important that you take that risk. When we lack museum directors, music festival managers and business leaders who dare to be in the vanguard with the risk of failing or being dismissed, things look pretty bad for our values.

To engage as much people in the indicated direction as possible, your communication has to be crystal clear. You can make your values explicit without attributing these values and characteristics to certain social groups: beware of duality! You communicate about people as individuals. In the example of the museum this means you tell that you do not comply with the request to cover the nudes, and you avoid speaking here about 'Muslims' in general terms. After all, the request was not made by 'Muslims,' you received this request from your own government on the occasion of the visit of a strict Islamic prime minister. Many Muslims in your own country will appreciate that you prevent stigmatization of all Muslims and it can motivate them to join you in your decision. Your guiding mix is then for example:

- Freedom of artistic expressions in the past and present is our core value.

- Welcome to visitors from all parts of the world who respect this value.

- Dialogue with your own government and (strictly religious) people who are uncomfortable with this value.

In the case of the music festival, you can say, for example, that there is no required format for songs submitted nor regulations for the texts and that you prefer countries to offer submissions that cannot be considered offensive by other countries. If you choose to handle it like this, the guiding mix would also consist of freedom of artistic expressions and dialogue; besides that, you give direction to the atmosphere and the framework conditions that you want for the festival.

In the example of the Middle East assignment, you probably say as little as possible; experience shows that little information is disclosed about this kind of situations but that they are met with quite some probing in-house questioning. For human resources policy, it forms a real test case of D&I: Therefore, you will need an open dialogue in all freedom. You might lose employees because you do not give in to the client and lose the assignment, thus needing to dismiss some employees. Or you might lose employees because you do give in and some of them are so shocked about it that they leave the company. In the case that you engage in a process of wheeling and dealing with the client, these employees will leave the company anyway certainly when other jobs are easily available because it disappoints them. Whatever you do, you need to be able to explain what you do and why and to take into consideration that a moment of public accountability will follow. A crystal clear and publishable choice would be the guiding mix with the core value of diversity, inclusion and non-discrimination and, if the client approves, with dialogue and for example a promise of outstanding performance above average that makes it extra attractive for the client to do business with you anyway.

THE ELEMENTS OF THE GUIDING MIX

There is no standard guiding mix for the dynamics of the 21st century. Every situation demands its own search for the right mix. Just look back at the example of the city of Cologne or the observation on diversity in jurisdiction; in both cases the wrong mix was chosen. With a different mix, there would have been other consequences and other, much more positive results. Also, a fast improvement to an adjusted mix could have worked. In any case, the secret of inclusive leadership is not to rely on an old and familiar mix. Dilemmas, ambiguities, and uncertainties force leaders to learn continuously and to open up to a new mix.

Guiding Mix for Inclusive Leadership	
Element	*Examples*
Value with long term validity.	Freedom of artistic expression. Equality of all employees.
Process that is followed to discuss or deal with the issue.	Dialogue. Developing solutions together. Look for connection, stay in touch. The interpersonal tone is professional.
Principle that defines the process and/or culture.	Discrimination-free work environment. Let a party be a party. A design for all. The judge rules.
Characteristic	*Examples*
Crystal clear.	Every employee and/or the stakeholders understand what it is about, why it matters and where it goes
Convincing.	Employees and/or the stakeholders feel involved in the value that is presented for the organization and see consistency and authenticity with the inclusive leader.

Especially, communication aspects require the inclusive leader's attention. This book shows numerous examples about the need to explain the guiding mix in the public domain: in the media, to politicians, to the general public. The average manager or director has not been trained for that purpose, nevertheless at unexpected moments it can suddenly become part of the job. To be crystal clear and convincing in the heat of the moment, that is not an easy task. However, chief of police Aalbersberg succeeded for one of the trickiest themes in the Netherlands during the last years. He provides an inspiring example that it can be done!

CHAPTER 4

Role Model Behavior

Seba Inclusive Leadership Model

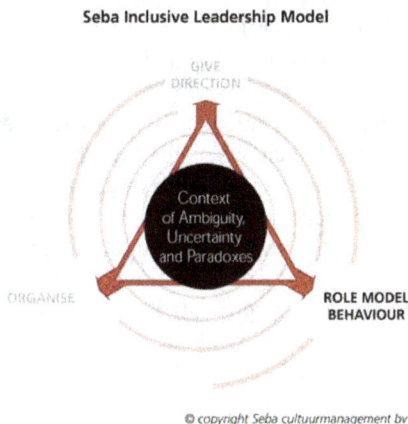

© copyright Seba cultuurmanagement bv

'Practice what you preach': you can hear it so often. And it applies more than average to inclusive leadership. A leader who wants to see inclusion in the organization must show role model behavior. Leading by example is another frequently heard motto that is suitable when striving for inclusive behavior.

In the publication *Get a Grip on Culture and Behavior*, PriceWaterhouseCoopers states: "Culture is shaped by the messages employees receive from the corporate leadership about the behavior that is appreciated in day-to-day reality. Hence this is not just about nice words, but mainly about acts: do as you say, walk the talk. 'Talk' without 'walk' will be counterproductive. Internal and external stakeholders easily notice the nature of that behavior."

Here, PWC makes a few very accurate statements:

- First of all, employees have a very well-developed internal indicator about the appreciation of behavior by the leadership. Employees usually discern clearly what the formal criteria are and what the genuine day-to-day evaluation is. The news that this often deviates does not come as a surprise. Think, for example, of the leader who states that he or she finds it very important for the organization to have employees with a critical attitude but whose direct surrounding is filled with yes-men. Or the leader who says that it is very important to have a diverse staff and then for every appointment under his or her responsibility, choose uniformity.

- Second, that employees tend to behave according to the deviation and not according to the formal norms. Hence, there are some executive directors who indicate that human capital is the most precious capital of the organization, demanding a careful approach and development. In the meantime, it is no exception that executive directors shout (!) to their employees in personal 'conversations.' Instead of the careful approach and development, it is the rude treatment that is copied organization-wide.

- Third, that organizations are worse off when they say one thing but do the other, then when they simply do not say anything at all. When 'they notice the nature of behavior,' a gap opens between the leadership and the stakeholders. The leadership meets with difficulties to implement targets because they lost credibility. Everybody knows organizations where people just shrug off 'the next plan' leaders present: it is 'talk without walk,' they couldn't care less. When it is about measurable targets, such as financial targets, the leadership still has the possibility to meet with this reaction, i.e. impose the targets through the systems of the organization. However, for desired behavior, the objectives set are impossible to achieve because they cannot be imposed.

- Fourth, that it is about internal and external stakeholders. In the current transparent times, the winds of the outside world regularly blow right through organizations. That outside world sees annual reports and websites just like before but also culture, the behavior and the diverse manifestations of all kind of employees are observed. This is an important insight for all organizations, whether they depend on consumers or patients, on stock exchange listing or on public opinion and appreciation: role model behavior of the leadership or the lack of it has a great influence on the confidence external stakeholders have in the organization. And in many cases, the reality is this: that these external stakeholders are much more diverse than the workforce of organizations. Winning confidence and realizing the right external image as desired by the company is a huge task in the current times of transparency and diversity.

In the last chapter, I described inclusive leadership from the point of view giving direction. The examples here above show just how important role model behavior is as a pillar of the triangle of inclusive leadership. In this chapter, I fill in the notion of 'inclusive role model behavior' for leaders with ambition. I turn it into a workable and applicable notion. As a guideline for it, I use the Seba Star of Inclusive Exemplary Behavior.

The Seba Star of Inclusive Exemplary Behaviour

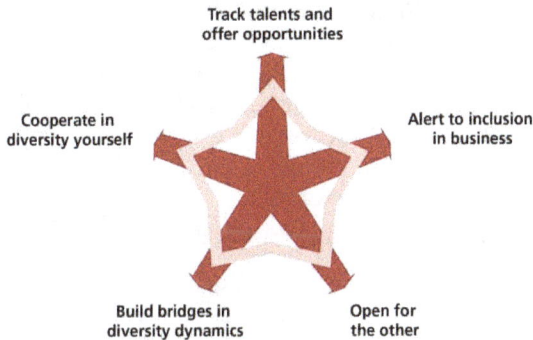

© copyright Seba cultuurmanagement bv

1. Track Talents and Offer Opportunities

It has been researched a thousand times and it has been an acknowledged fact for many years: people appreciate people who resemble them more, than people with different characteristics or qualities. Indeed, the difference can interfere so strongly in the contact that it limits their perceptions of the talents that 'other' persons bring. The color of their glasses gets in the way. This is why organizations are inclined to constantly appoint and reward the same social type of people. 'Cloning' is another term for this phenomenon. Recognizing and valuing diversity seems to be directly opposed to the daily reality at work. Thus, the ambition for inclusion, when people can be their own unique self and contribute to the whole because they belong, is not automatically transferred in behavior that has inclusion as a result. It is important to note that this is a general mechanism and not a matter of personal ill will. The approach of 'guilt and expiation' that we can often see in the field of D&I is not effective. What is effective is when leaders choose to adopt this mechanism as their personal responsibility. Make sure that you recognize and identify the mechanism of cloning; understand that an inclusive organization demands active ownership.

> One must dare to appoint people who are very different. Of course, explanation is needed when such appointments are made. Also discuss uncertainty, inclusive leadership means that leaders dare to be vulnerable.
>
> Fawzia Nasrullah, CEO youthcare institution Youké

Another aspect is that people show their talents in many different ways. Some do that *assertively*, even though assertiveness in itself is a subjective concept. After all, whoever is seen as assertive in the Netherlands, will come across as modest in the United States. Others show their talent by hard work and deep commitment without singing the praises about their own achievements. Then there is a group whose talents are much more than their self-confidence. They live with the permanent doubt that their contribution is not sufficient, even though it is better than others. This goes for example for the highly gifted because their high intelligence often allows them to see what is still lacking and it makes them insecure. Organizations that wait and see what talents automatically knock at their door risk to get too much of the same and let's be honest, that is what happens on a massive scale.

> At this moment, we need to be careful with the hype of working with management drives or similar team and management tests. Management drives classes of people in colors and says something about personal drives, strengths and pitfalls. For an initial awareness, it serves as a nice way to look at yourself and the group. In education for example you see a lot of employees who are first and foremost driven by the development of people. However, there is a risk of prompt judgement: 'I am green and I go for orange now.' People can talk about their colors all too enthusiastically because passion and talent are colorblind. In practice, there is the risk that it becomes an unsolicited stamp on people's heads.
> Leadership means that you do what is asked from you in specific situations and such a test cannot say anything about that. To really scout talent, you have to reflect on the spot on the horizon, to foster development and movement and to make a profile that fits with that. For example, the Amsterdam Economic Board started working with connectors, I found that an eye-catcher: Making a connection is more important than claiming a position! Hence you will meet with totally different talent, via a completely different process than when you are the 'coordinator.' Moving and connecting beat the positional play. If you can't move and connect, you will not be able to find new talent.
>
> Marij Urlings, director Domain Education & Innovation, Inholland University of Applied Sciences

Inclusive exemplary behavior means that leaders themselves engage in tracking diverse talents and offering opportunities. A leader that preaches D&I while appointing in practice mainly clones of him or herself creates the old, uniform workplace that suited in the past. A firm belief that everybody has unique talents and that everybody is needed will work fine when accompanied by concrete appointments to show that business works differently for the 21st century than in the past. Of course, this means also a risk for the organization as a whole and specifically for those who were involved in the nomination of 'new social types.' Leaders somehow make their mark with the people who are appointed under their responsibility. If these people do not 'succeed,' it has a negative effect on the leaders. By appointing people who are in one way or the other just different or who are perceived as a different social type by others, leaders are not just dependent of their own guidance to make this appointment work but also of the extent to which these 'others' are able to cooperate in a team where colleagues differ from each other.

That is the reason why 'different' candidates who are the first to be appointed because of D&I policies usually have to be very, very good. These candidates must be good experts in their field and capable to overcome eventual problems in cooperation or even certain negative perceptions about themselves. Is that honest, no, it probably isn't. During the years there have been many surveys that show the existence of this reality. They led to a lot of discussion though there is no way to avoid this reality through 'more honesty' and the like. A more effective approach is to recognize that this is the way it works and to develop a long-term vision that is strongly connected to the already-diverse society. Uniformity is or seems to be absence of risk at short notice. With a bit of luck, the 'bill' for lack of vision and insights in D&I is only presented to the organization under the next leader. Tracking diverse talents and offering opportunities demand courageous leaders who dare to look across their own leadership period and feel responsible for that. D&I reduces the long-term risks that definitively exist for organizations and offers new opportunities when the workforce is able to cooperate within an inclusive culture.

This paragraph is deliberately described in a rather gloomy than cheerful tone of voice. After decades of D&I policies with limited results, we can continue to praise the blessings of D&I in organizations but it is good to face realistically that people just find D&I difficult. They are hardly convinced by beautiful stories. This state of affairs screams for leadership. When Paul Polman took office as CEO at Unilever, few people talked about the ecological footprint. Polman proved that it is possible to turn around a worldwide company for a transformation whose legitimacy nobody denies nowadays. At Unilever, this process is combined with a strong policy for D&I because the transformation to a sustainable organization has everything to do with large and deep roots in the diverse society. It is not a coincidence that the credo of sustainability is *people, planet, profit.*

Common perceptions are that people is about needy people like in the textile industry in Bangladesh and not about the people who work in modern companies and live in well-developed countries. Think about this however: how credible is it to start actions for the needy in poor countries and in the same time exclude people from cooperation or promotion for certain functions in one's own organization? Sustainability concerns materials, environment and also the people within and around the organization. That is not easy, but it is really necessary. It does not improve the quarterly figures, but it does improve the annual figures in the longer term. It meets with resistance in organizations because people who belong to a 'uniform' social group experience this as unfair competition. That is why leadership is of vital importance and tracking talents and offering opportunities form the top of the Seba Star of Inclusive Exemplary Behavior.

2. Cooperate in Diversity Yourself

> It is a challenge to also cooperate in diversity yourself. The moment you are part of an oil tanker, you yourself will also show its characteristics: slow, bureaucratic, with a lot of rules and consultative structures. You do not preserve a world that is diverse but a world that looks like the oil tanker. And this is how you measure performance and behavior. Surely, this is a road with dead end. There is not enough room for questions of clients and the environment.
>
> We have to organize more in neighbourhoods and in the region. Slowly we move into another direction. Within a foreseeable time, education is a completely different setting with a diverse range of teachers and public. A well worked out knowledge and (local) moral agenda as well as the co-creation with parents, students and teachers will hopefully have utmost influence on all 'state solutions' that are now lugged into the education system.
>
> Marij Urlings, director Domain Education & Innovation, Inholland University of Applied Sciences

Many leaders reside in an ivory tower of uniformity. Both internally and externally, there are many contacts with 'similar' people. Sex, age, culture, religion or belief, educational background and living area: the higher you get in organizations, the more resemblances seem to exist. 'Seem' because in recent years more and more stories pop up of people who 'get off.' They start to consider the requirements to advance professionally as a sacrifice of themselves, of their identity. Or like a female top manager told me: 'Every evening when I came home, I needed more time to just become myself again and I thought: I don't want this anymore.' After almost twenty years of investment she could be admitted to the top of the organization as partner and she decided not to do so. Such a choice is no longer an exception but an increasing trend.

Inclusive role model behavior means that you as a leader meet and cooperate with diverse social types of people yourself. When you do not have them around you automatically, organize it. Leaders who promote the creation of inclusive teams but never deal with diversity in teams themselves are unconvincing theorists. Indeed, in theory it looks wonderful and creative to work with different people but in practice it often leads to a longer period of habituation. The risk of thinking in terms of us-them is real. Also managing of diverse teams initially appears to be much more complicated than expected.

How diverse are the teams you work with on a daily basis? Do you create the conditions for inclusive teams or are you one of those leaders who 'does not see the problem' when there are signals from the work floor that diverse colleagues do not get on well and that it is not that simple altogether? Be a hero and step personally into the world of cooperation in diversity. Experience in day-to-day activities the advantages of differences between colleagues including the challenging situations. I am absolutely certain that leaders who work with a diversity of colleagues on a day-to-day basis respond differently to discussions about painful matters like Zwarte Piet than leaders who reside mainly in their safe tower of uniformity. And this also goes for discussions about the observation of one minute's silence at work after terror attacks, for discussions about the (im)possibility to cooperate with the colleagues who were added to the department after a merger, the discussion about quota for (top)women or the ambition to come up with multidisciplinary solutions. The leader who is a living example of teamwork in diversity for better and worse becomes an authority and speaks with authority and has substantial impact on the creation of an inclusive organization.

Last but not least in this part of the Seba Star of Inclusive Exemplary Behavior: do not forget to review with a critical eye the young people who fulfill roles in your direct surroundings. Many leaders have one or more secretaries, personal assistants, a communication advisor and the like who are not necessarily appointed by leaders themselves but who often do show a striking mutual resemblance. It is embarrassing and usually not accepted to say this outright. However, awareness starts by facing reality. One leader is surrounded by a group of people in their twenties and thirties who all have a background in specific student associations. Another leader is surrounded by beautiful young guys or even beautiful Asian women. Yet another leader has not a single person under the age of 45 in his support team.

'What a good copier they have here,' someone told me with a wink when we had another of these experiences at a visit on the 20th floor. Exemplary behavior means that you notice and that you take the lead in this. Believe me indeed, when this is the case at your workplace, quite some people in the organization have already noticed and they talk about it among themselves. They express controversial interpretations that you do not want to hear and that are most probably wrong. Break through the stereotypes and avoid reproaches that the copier at your floor works better than in any other floor of the organization.

3. Alert to Inclusion in Business

If you want all project managers, developers and designers in the organization to work inclusively for the customers, then it is important to show role model behavior and make remarks at proposals offered to you, to foster inclusion in business. Quite often products and services are still developed on the basis of a general norm that is moreover not really 'general' but rooted in a traditional target group of mindsets. For example, a while ago, I was present at a viewing day of a major housing project with the responsible project manager. In earlier presentations of the project I had already indicated that they always worked with one-sided images of future inhabitants: a white man and woman with two children, a boy and a girl. At the viewing day, a lot of the viewers appeared to be couples with Moroccan and Turkish background in their thirties. 'Do these people really have this kind of money?' the project manager asked me with surprise. 'Of course,' I said because who could have missed that the progress the parents strived for our children will have a better life that we had is often accomplished in reality? 'Yeah, but so many of them,' he added. Yes, they were many; nevertheless few houses were sold to them. The reason for that was not a lack of money. It was the layout of the house that did not meet with their expectations although it concerned a neighbourhood where they'd love to live. It took the project manager quite a while to sell his houses to good buyers and he made a lot less profit than he could have made with a more visionary approach.

> In our context, we start new projects with diversity as integral component from the start. But at the end only 40 percent of what we figured out, remains. Surely to start again makes no sense. For example, a new way of working for teachers in the future: when it is developed by a small group, ownership is not accepted by the people who are going to carry it out. Experience has shown us that the innovative power diversity offers at the beginning dilutes when many people join. The dot on the horizon is that people really *feel* ownership, that their influence is clear. That is essential for a good long-term implementation. When that feeling lacks, people revert to their old ways in which they feel safe because that is what they already know.
>
> Marij Urlings, director Domain Education & Innovation, Inholland University of Applied Sciences

For some products and services, adjusting at the end is difficult or even impossible. Therefore, the inclusive approach has to be part of it from the beginning. When you design a building, it is cleverer to think of the accessibility for people with disabilities right from the start. Adjustments afterwards are difficult and expensive. Moreover, the accessibility problems create a lot of societal resistance in case of a public building. We also know the history of medication that was only tested on white males with all the resulting consequences for women and people with different racial background. And who has never come across the difficulty ICT-systems have with the fact that family names within families can differ and that not only men but also women can be the applicant of a mortgage or insurance and particularly with the inalterability of those ICT-systems. Another example is that of children's toys that do not focus on the competences of the individual child but on the supposed masculinity or femininity of the child and the desired role that comes with it while playing. Real movements of parents were set up against that such as 'Let Toys Be Toys.' Even in education often the child's gender is still more preponderant for role distribution than the child's competences. In many countries, hotlines have started to report stereotypes in schoolbooks. In the Netherlands, where all LGBTQ rights are equal by law, we still find it very difficult to ensure inclusive shelter and health care: in asylum centers as well as in care for the elderly special projects are started for LGBTQ people because otherwise their safety and free identity is threatened. For all these cases, reflection about it only started when the problems occurred. What is missing is a design for all beforehand!

> All our efforts mainly concentrate on training judges to communicate with everybody and to deal with very different situations. As a judge, you have to switch between all kinds of people during a long afternoon and often this goes perfectly well. As for the content of jurisdiction there is sometimes deepening for example concerning honor crimes: such cultural elements are thoroughly studied. Not that they are accepted, but they are evaluated in the light of our task. The problem of the more severe punishment (Note: see page 45) goes for everybody. A lot of importance is attached to the possibility to retain a job. That this creates problems in practice because people with a migrant background are punished more heavily does not make the measure itself unfair. A problem is also that we do not maintain statistics about it because we do not register according to ethnicity. It is not because a person is indigenous or migrant but because society is unequal.
>
> A measure that has a disproportionate outcome does lead to discussion: is it not strange that we act like this with such an effect? But that does not necessarily lead to a different way of acting because the objective norm is still having a job; regardless the ethnic background. If you stay as objective as possible, officially you do not see it and the effect of that objectivity is that nothing changes. We do not consider the effect on the whole; we do not take that into account in specific crime cases.
>
> I would say this is obviously an example of the context of ambiguity, uncertainty and paradoxes.
>
> Willem Korthals Altes, senior judge Court of Amsterdam and chair complaints committee National Police

This also goes for major policy moves like the development of the Smart Cities as mentioned in the introduction. The city of the future is developed from a technical point of view and after that the effects for social cohesion and inclusion are studied. A real Smart City is smart and contains inclusion from the beginning. Indeed, designs are not without limitations and developments are often disruptive but it does really make an essential difference whether inclusion is in the heads of leaders and designers at every step taken or whether inclusion is introduced afterwards as a kind of repair agent for a tire that in fact was punctured already in the production phase.

Be a living example of *design for all* for your people. Ask questions and do not allow proposals to pass without real strategic decision making in terms of inclusion.

4. Build Bridges in Diversity Dynamics

Twynstra Gudde initiated a study in 2011 on new leadership and phrased the conclusion as followed:

> "In the 'new' leadership, cooperation with people to reach objectives is more central than in the 'old' leadership, where the focus was on organizing tasks and processes. In this 'old' vision, the leader had the role as director and as a 'wall' that protected the company from the unpredictable world outside. Now that the world outside is increasingly turbulent, that has become an *idée fixe*. The leader can no longer get things done on his own in the organization or in

the outside world. The transfer to the internal organization namely lies in line with what is happening outside. That produces all kinds of questions leaders see themselves confronted with. The answer that results from this study points in the direction of the ability of the leader to build bridges and to find the right balance between inside and outside.'[5]

Leader in a balancing act is what the authors call it in a different place in the same article. All the time, I observe that today's context is a different, more complex context than the one in the 20th century.

> When you really know how to build bridges, people will start to move.
>
> Fawzia Nasrullah, CEO youthcare institution Youké

Sometimes interests are clearly opposites. For example, for COA, the Dutch national organization for the shelter of asylum seekers, it is considerably cheaper to work with large scale shelters of hundreds, maybe even thousands of places at one location. In the meantime, more and more local governments plead to have small-scale accommodation because this improves the local support to house asylum seekers as well as their integration in Dutch society. However, the long-term fruits of such an approach which include cost savings by good integration would not return to the COA themselves.

Also, quite often there is uncertainty about the right interpretation of events. There are dilemmas and there is the big issue of the potential clash of values. Diversity dynamics put relationships under pressure. Rightly, the article shows that there is no longer an outside world on the other side of the walls of the organization. The outside world enters the organization from all sides, expresses opinions, and has demands that employees might find impossible but that doesn't change the facts. To be a connecting leader in this balancing act means spending a lot of time with all different parties and stakeholders. What helps is to know as a leader what dot on the horizon you are heading for. And even that dot on the horizon can be unclear and even then, you can be a bridge building leader if you work with the guiding mix as discussed in the last chapter. Some examples:

a. You are a school leader in primary education and parents have started an action because they see too much traditional male-female patterns at your school. They think the school books and other materials are role-enforcing and that this also goes for the way your staff treats the boys and the girls. The teachers for the youngest children are all female, for the higher classes they are mixed male-female and you yourself as a school leader are a man. It is a difficult task for you to change it all at once in a month time but on the other

---

[5] (Turbulent times ask for connecting leadership, published (in Dutch) on www.kluwermanagement.nl article code 0179, by Roline Roos, Martijn Jansen and Britta Gielen)

hand the pressure is strong because the parents of the new action group have approached the newspaper already. A counter-movement has started too: the traditional Christian constituency of the school is not pleased by the actions.

b. You are mayor of a Dutch local community with a shelter for asylum seekers. There are signals that gay asylum seekers face mobbing and threats. Not just you yourself, also the majority of your council think that asylum seekers need to adjust to the Dutch laws, norms and values and that the behavior of the attackers is unacceptable. Not the gay refugees must be sheltered in a special place but those who misbehaved should be set apart and eventually expelled from the country. That is a clear viewpoint; however the responsible organizations such as the COA and the police do not seem to get a good grip on the problems. In the meantime, the pressure from LGBTQ groups and public opinion increases to offer better shelter for gay refugees.

c. You run a chain of restaurants for fast food with low prices for the customers. Among your customers are many families with smaller budgets. There is quite some societal pressure on the fast food industry because the food is allegedly unhealthy. Right or wrong, your expectation is that this negative press will influence the company's turnover and hence the results. In your management team irritations about the anti-lobby for fast food dominate; they feel that the lobby is mainly held by people who have enough money to pay for much more expensive food. However, not everybody has the money to visit restaurants of class. Moreover, market surveys among customers indicate that the great majority is happy with what is actually offered.

d. You work in the world of employment agencies. Public opinion blames you for only interceding for the middle group: the employees with at least a number of years of work experience, not too young, not too old, indigenous rather than migrants and without disabilities. Indeed, it is correct that your agencies serve relatively more employees of this type but you carefully avoid handing over this kind of figures. Because this is the type of employee that your customers ask for. Your critics want you to convince your customers and create more openness for diverse types of employees. Your risk is that these customers might go to a competitor who offers them what they say they need without wasting their time with discussions about things they do not want.

To build bridges in diversity dynamics does not mean that you have the answers to all these situations. Even the guiding mix might probably not derive from your personal ideas but from the dialogue with employees, advisors and stakeholders. In the cases above, you are building bridges in the middle of diversity dynamics when you show in your words and behavior that you want to achieve a good outcome in contact with or even in cooperation with the different parties and stakeholders involved. To do so, you can have a modest start like 'after all it must be possible that we work this out together' or express ambitions like 'in the end we work towards results such as.'

In any case, connecting leadership means that you do not fear diversity dynamics and are even capable to encourage it. Allow the diverse perspectives and methods to be presented. Make sure people listen to each other and have a dialogue. Recognize people's uniqueness and show trust within the context of the larger interest that they all feel involved with: the school where every child with its own character can learn and develop as needed; the shelter where every asylum seeker can stay in safety, the affordable restaurant with good food, the employment agency that offers job opportunities to all.

> Building bridges is the magic word here. When you listen to the Mayor of Rotterdam Aboutaleb (who has Moroccan roots), you are in connection with his heritage, maybe because he is a world citizen.
> Reflectivity is the most beautiful ability one can have. For me, analysis and reflection go together. They are directly related to yourself as a person and your behavior as a leader. Share issues with a diverse range of people, involve them, dare to ask. The more you reflect, the more your impact is and like that you can also achieve more to create movement in situations. People with guts do that *on the edge,* I do not think that I myself work like that yet. People with guts find a fracture surface in a development and use it to make a jump. That driver is a prelude for inclusion. You know how to use it for yourself and it is impossible for you not to see it with others and encourage them to use it too.
>
> Marij Urlings, director Domain Education & Innovation, Inholland University of Applied Sciences

This lies far from the old leadership, resumed in the article of Twynstra Gudde mentioned above as 'organizing tasks and processes.' In fact, that old leadership is much closer to management than to leadership as I showed in the chapter 'Give Direction': 'Giving direction is what distinguished a leader from a manager.' The leader does not work on his or her own; neither is the leader protecting the organization from the mean world outside. Rightly, the authors of the article state that it is about the ability of the leader to connect and to find the right balance between the world inside and outside. For those who still consider the organization of tasks and processes as the main job to do, this connecting role is a vague and elusive process. However, for those who want to make the difference in actual education, public administration, or business life: for those leaders seeking and realizing connections are vital to obtain results.

Inclusive Leadership is practiced by showing vulnerability and by being vulnerable. That works out positively for the organization, as the job satisfaction survey shows when we ask to what extent employees experience space to move, to shape their development, to take off. We score differently from other parts of the Defense organization. Surely our work is more individual but still the organization seems to be more cohesive. The other side is that when colleagues clearly oppose themselves to the organization, this is felt as if it were personal. A colleague who takes distance easily becomes exclusive.

Vulnerability means that as a leader you feel the freedom to say: 'at this moment, I do not know.' You will then see many helping hands, instead of opinions about your proposal or viewpoint. The effect is a larger participation in the things you are doing. Still vulnerability is a threshold because it does not meet with the stereotype of 'strong leaders' that everybody asks for at the moment. The strength of vulnerability has not at all been discovered yet.

The risk is that new leaders mainly want to decide themselves, in an environment where people increasingly ask questions about the correctness of decisions made. Through participation and mutual agreement, the support is far greater. To show that you are there for colleagues, also as human being, is much stronger than to push visibly for everybody all sorts of buttons and handles. Sharing doubts is much stronger than informing how the world works, nobody believes that any more.

André Peperkoorn, deputy commander Royal Netherlands Marechaussee

5. Open for the Other

Most leaders see themselves preferably as open, accessible and good receivers of feedback. However, they have limitations that cannot always be understood rationally. First, a general example of this:

> *Ian fulfilled an interim assignment in an organization where the processes did not run smoothly. It was Ian's assignment to achieve a better process alignment in consultation with all parties involved in the organization. Thus, the goals of the organization would be achieved more easily and the costs would go down. Full of enthusiasm, he started to work and got cooperation of all colleagues. One colleague in particular, Peter, was very enthusiast but less talented in processes. Peter had a management position and as such he continuously thwarted the remedial actions Ian launched. He always reacted cheerfully when Ian confronted him but nothing changed. That is why Ian mailed his client, Dennis, the company's CEO, that it didn't work like this and something should be done about it. Consequently, Dennis decided to remove Ian from a part of the assignment: 'Because this is not the way we do things here,' Dennis said.*

This example may sound irrational, but, alas, it is not unfamiliar at all. In seemingly innocent situations, the expression of feedback and the question for improvement, regardless the good intentions, lead to a less favorable assessment and even exclusion. Ian encountered one of the invisible rules organizations often have—rules that determine the culture and thus at least partly the possibilities for a good result. In this case, the unwritten rule was that no one should criticize that particular manager. Everybody knew that but nobody warned Ian about it. Officially, this rule did not exist but when Ian's assignment was curtailed, from several sides, he got explanations about why that happened: 'How could you be so stupid, they go on holidays together,' or 'I don't exactly know but I think Peter knows too much about Dennis so Dennis cannot do anything about him.' Ian was recruited to bring change and when that change appeared to have a relation with other matters than thought of beforehand, Dennis withdrew. Dennis did want things to improve, but at the core, he was not open to the other, be it either Ian's working method or the consequences of his remedial actions. He closed the door in a painful way for Ian. As said, organizations have limitations that cannot always be understood rationally.

D&I is specifically at risk because practice proves the themes that come with them a high probability of provoking irrationality. When the doors that seemed to stand wide open with Dennis already close when it is about process improvement by someone recruited externally, how will things turn out for the internal employee who tells the leader that:

- The design of a new product that is almost ready for market, is not a design for all;

- He saw that a manager discriminates against an employee or shows sexist behavior;

- The organization denies its core values through measure X, Y or Z;

- People who have disabilities or who are transgender do not get any real chances in the organization?

As said, most leaders like to see themselves as open, accessible and good receivers of feedback. Let the statements above sink in one by one and reflect on how you or leaders around you would react on them.

Inclusive leadership needs a great ability to receive feedback and handle many antennas. Truly listening to different social types of people is a major challenge. Our society is making progress but there are still male leaders who have difficulty to communicate with women and conversely, female leaders who mainly feel at ease with their female managers. To be open for the other is strongly tested in diversity dynamics. Think again of the example above and replace Ian by Caroline: does that make a difference? Or in another variety, the interim professional's name is now Caroline but Peter is called Mohamed and Dennis Khalid, both have Arab roots. What diversity dynamics can now be perceived in the case? Remarks like 'How could you be so stupid, they go on holidays together' or 'I don't exactly know but I think Mohamed knows too much about Khalid, so Khalid cannot do anything about him' may have a different significance with Peter and Dennis than with Mohamed and Khalid. If that is not how your perceptions work, be sure that it does indeed go for a number of your colleagues. And if we let Dennis to stay just Dennis but Peter is now Mohamed, the dynamics are different again.

Having the ability to listen truly to your interlocutor regardless the social type is a first step. It becomes even better when the inclusive leader not only shows the ability to encourage the diverse contributions of the interlocutors but also to appreciate them by including them in situations where normally just the point of view of the majority prevails. Building on the example above:

> *That is why Ian emailed his client Dennis, the company's CEO, that it didn't work like this and something should be done about it. Dennis entered into dialogue with Ian and asked all sorts of questions about the things he had encountered. Then Dennis brought to Ian's attention that Ian mainly brought him problems and no solutions. 'If I had the solution, I would not need to send you an email,' Ian responded. He could not be moved to talk to Peter because he tried that already. Finally, Dennis decides to enter into dialogue with Peter and Ian together. Ian is not allowed to interrupt Peter and Peter shall sincerely consider Ian's objections. This shows that Peter can no longer deliver his work for specific customers in a too-tight process structure; these customers are so-called key accounts that do not fit into a standard process. The next question Ian asks is, of course, what process improvement he is expected to achieve. His assignment is evaluated and adjusted with a number of colleagues in the light of the requirements set by the business. Both Ian and Peter can live with these results. Some problematic issues and apparent inconsistencies remain; they agree on continuation of the dialogue about them.*

When Ian is Caroline and Peter and Dennis are Mohamed and Khalid, then this approach will have similar effects, even though the dynamics differ. If Khalid succeeds to involve Caroline and Mohamed in an open dialogue with each other about the business, then he will develop into an inclusive leader. It is an inevitable reality that Khalid might have to walk over more risky or complex paths than a Dennis in the same position, but Khalid's exceptional ethnic background is not new to him and previous balanced ways of handling that eventually brought him to the CEO position he holds now.

Does the example also go when it is about work-related issues of D&I instead of process improvement? Yes, it does and it certainly helps if the organization has an inclusive leader who considers D&I themes the same way as business issues like process improvement. Suppose the organization follows a route to have more inclusive teams. That demands an approach quite different from the traditional one everybody is used to. Ian finds Peter's way difficult and turns to Dennis. Why not discuss this in a similar way? And here again, other dynamics appear when we replace

Ian by Caroline and Peter and Dennis by Mohamed and Khalid or only Peter by Mohamed. What the dynamics will be does not only depend on these three persons, their characters and the perceptions they might have about social types, but also on other colleagues in the organization who each have their own perceptions. From the Seba Star of Inclusive Exemplary Behavior both Dennis and Khalid will need the quality of 'build bridges in diversity dynamics' next to 'open to the other.' This is how consistent and recognizable exemplary behavior is shown for the appreciation and inclusion of diverse contributions.

The example even goes when it is about the leader personally and his or her behavior, for example when an employee thinks that the leader is discriminating and is bold enough to tell him so. This kind of situation is a well-known recipe to make leaders lose their head and fiercely go on the defensive, but that is not an unavoidable matter-of-fact. Surely leaders know themselves whether they intend to discriminate or not. If they don't, why not let the employee explain quietly and ask more questions and listen to the perceptions that arose. Why do you experience it this way? What in my actions or behavior brought that up? Whatever the outcome of the discussion will be, with this kind of openness and accessibility it will certainly evolve differently than with the closed reaction of denial and defense.

Ideally, it is a conscious strategy of the inclusive leader to create more dynamics through openness and accessibility. Diverse perspectives and ideas contribute to the results of the organization, provided that they are utilized and if possible that they can interact and even conflict for a while. The Netherlands are the country of the 'poldermodel' and that has many advantages. They are good at negotiating and giving everybody his or her own share. Where in other countries people still struggle with contrasts, the Dutch have already worked out the compromise. However, it made them less able to support eventual conflicting viewpoints. As soon as a conflict seems to occur, it is already concealed. Nevertheless, organizations can profit from a bit of conflict under inclusive leadership of course. 'There is no polish without friction' says an old Dutch proverb. In case the problem is that diversity dynamics challenge the necessary processes of business operations, then radically change the organizational structure.

This is what Atilla Aytekin does for Orange Games. He observes that start-ups have difficulty to flourish in existing organizations because they contain often wild ideas or initiatives that cross right through the indispensable processes. The risk of suffocation is already there before anything could have arisen at all. Moreover, he found out that people who are good in start-ups and initial growth are rarely the same people as those who lead a full-grown company towards the next step. Indeed, the first group is the managing entrepreneurs and the second group is the entrepreneurial managers. In fact, this is common knowledge to entrepreneurs, managers and policy makers. Atilla Aytekin is not just open in the sense that he opens up for such information, he is also the first entrepreneur in the Netherlands to start his own campus where all types of people can flourish in their own unique way.

Business life is a very international environment. Already your own employees show an enormous variety. Moreover, there are good employees with new ideas and products and you think: will that person stay in my company or start a business for himself or herself? That is thinking in hostile views and threats. Of course, you can protect yourself but not too much indeed because in doing so you will kill the entrepreneurship. If nobody develops new ideas, there will be no competitive new businesses and there will be no growth. This is why we choose for a connecting growth strategy. As Orange Games, we start our own campus where the cycle of new products can evolve in unique ways. Thus, we give space to innovation within our own company. We divide the campus in start-ups. Start-ups get their first budgets to work with. Growers get a larger budget and cells are mature products with the organization around it. Also, we invite external parties to join because this problem exists in many corporates, that they cannot develop new ideas into mature growth. It gives incentives to employees instead of discouraging them. Whoever wants to try out an idea, can go to the start-ups on the second floor. It gives space to people who often get trapped in the existing organization.

Atilla Aytekin, CEO Orange Games

THE REVENUES OF EXEMPLARY BEHAVIOR

The five points of the Seba Star of Inclusive Exemplary Behavior ask a lot from you. The revenues largely compensate the efforts. Leaders who show exemplary behavior in practice meet with the positive effects and advantages of D&I in the organization. People follow a good example, it is really true. Imagine that an important part of the people around you show these behavioral characteristics in both word and deed.

The Seba Star of Inclusive Exemplary Behaviour

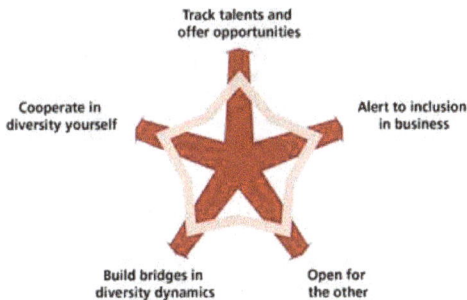

Track talents and offer opportunities

Cooperate in diversity yourself

Alert to inclusion in business

Build bridges in diversity dynamics

Open for the other

© copyright Seba cultuurmanagement bv

Your life will be so much easier. Of course, not everybody equally has every characteristic. And not every characteristic is equally important in the actual phase of your organization. Invest in the characteristics that matter most and you will certainly see the revenues of inclusive exemplary behavior.

CHAPTER 5

Organize: Managing Critical Success Factors

Seba Inclusive Leadership Model

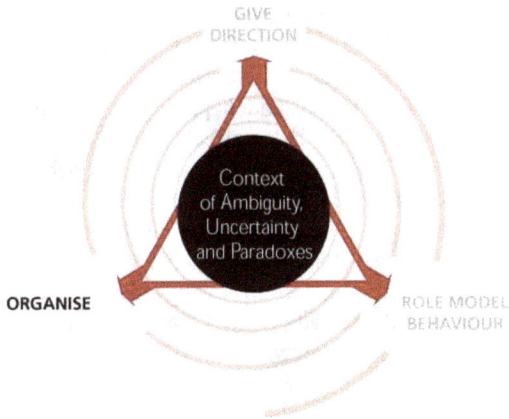

GIVE
DIRECTION

Context
of Ambiguity,
Uncertainty
and Paradoxes

ORGANISE

ROLE MODEL
BEHAVIOUR

© copyright Seba cultuurmanagement bv

- *A dress code for female officers at the city counters of Amsterdam bring about a real #rokjesgate ('skirtsgate') on Twitter, national news sites and broadcasting media and political questions in the national parliament.*

- *Warehouse Hema becomes national news because a communication officer states that Happy Easter is replaced by Happy Spring to prevent anybody to take offense.*

How does the local government of Amsterdam circa 2016 end up in a real #rokjesgate? How does the Dutch's most beloved warehouse Hema end up in an uncomfortable discussion about the use of the word Easter in their publicity? These are just two examples of what I call unmanaged diversity. Mind you, these two are both forerunners in the field of diversity. The government of Amsterdam has made efforts during many years for both a diverse staff and good ties with the large diversity of Amsterdam citizens and companies. Warehouse Hema succeeded in attracting and retaining a large diversity of customers by offering different products such as products for Eid, the Feast at the End of Ramadan in a time where no others offered comparable products yet. However, the same rule as always goes here: Results achieved in the past are no guarantee for the future. The developments related to D&I are dynamic and need to be ensured at all levels of the organization if you don't want to be overwhelmed with criticism on the internet and in national media, as what happened to the local government of Amsterdam and Warehouse Hema. As is so often the case, the strength of a chain is that of its weakest link.

Organizations that used to invest a lot in D&I in the past get new leaders who think 'D&I have had their day.' They want to engage in other issues. However, D&I cannot be 'finished'; this theme belongs as integral part to their regular work package and hopefully also to their luggage. The introduction of this book showed already that there are continuously new developments, not just because of the 'Middle East effects' on organizations but also because of the changing labor market and technological innovations. By lack of alertness, companies and institutions are completely taken by surprise by the sudden public and political attention and they suffer heavily from the negative publicity effects. Such situations prove whether the words of the leaders (the guiding mix) and the role model behavior of the leaders can also be found in the business operations of the organization. That is why organizing D&I is an important third aspect of the Seba Model for Inclusive Leadership next to giving direction and showing exemplary behavior. If you are not able to organize D&I effectively, the machine will hamper and you will find yourself at unwelcome moments in the media in a defensive position. My position is without leadership in D&I, it becomes political. That is a new phenomenon in this time and a development to take into account.

This chapter offers numerous tools through the method of ten critical success factors to concretely implement the management of diversity and create inclusion at all levels of your organization. There is no lack of professionals or methods to realize this. However, this does not go for the necessary time and resources; this is where shortage occurs. To have D&I as focus area or area of attention is not enough and will not do the job for you. As a leader, you do not need to do everything yourself, but you should know what is at stake and in what activities the organization can be engaged. You should be able to evaluate what is or is not going to work for the organization and the employees involved and facilitate the process with sufficient time and resources. This is how giving direction, showing exemplary behavior and organizing mutually reinforce each other so that even in a context of uncertainties, dilemmas and paradoxes you utilize the advantages of diversity for your organization.

TEN CRITICAL SUCCESS FACTORS: A BUSINESS METHODOLOGY FOR D&I

What should be at stake while organizing and what actions will be effective? This is why Seba developed the methodology of the ten critical success factors. Indeed, many actions can be started in view of diversity management: training, developing new methods for recruitment, having discussions about vision or form customer panels and so on. But what will bring you the best return on investment? Working with critical success factors supports you to have positive results for D&I. Before I separately focus on each single factor, I first elaborate on ways to work with this business methodology for D&I. Middle manager Peter who serves as a model in different steps, symbolizes the reactions and feelings leaders often encounter at the implementation of D&I.

Peter leads a policy department at the ministry. The department has a lot of contact with agriculture and horticulture organizations. The field of agriculture and horticulture is still formed by the traditional, native white inhabitants with a considerable part of strictly religious people. Until recently D&I was no issue at all for Peter's department, why deal with people with a migrant background? There is a certain staff turnover among the younger personnel. Peter who has worked at the ministry for over twenty years sees that people stay either just for a few years or they never leave at all. A middle group that would work between five and ten years at the ministry seems to be non-existent. This phenomenon has never been labeled as a diversity issue. As for men and women, Peter doesn't know exactly what the situation is: he doesn't signal any problems. In the field, man-woman issues do not play a significant role because it is rather traditional. New in the field however are the gay farmers who do make their voice heard. For Peter, it is not yet very clear what that is supposed to be, gay farming, and what the involvement of a policy department would be. But it is clear however that the field will be changing in the years to come.

Positive Action Alone: Is that Enough?

The first association many professionals have with organizing D&I is positive action (factor 9). Functions are reserved or preferably assigned to employees of a specific social type, for example women. The focus then lies on figures of recruitment and career advancement. Less attention is paid to the organizational culture (factor 2) or on skills to deal with differences (factor 5 or 6). That is why the effect of positive action alone on organizations is quite limited. The frequently praised and highly expected results of D&I remain disappointing, nevertheless the resistance against the subject increases. In uniformed organizations like the police and armies it has happened for example that the amount of women and employees with different ethnic background who were leaving the organization was higher than those coming in: 'the front door was wide open but so was the back door.' This turns positive action rather into desperate action. Neither the #rokjesgate (skirtgate) in Amsterdam and the Happy Easter/Happy Spring case at Warehouse Hema could have been prevented by applying positive action.

Peter had only one experience with an employee of Moroccan background. That was already a few years ago when it was a trend at the ministry to recruit more employees from different ethnic minorities. It was not a success: the man didn't have a clue about agriculture or horticulture. Also he overestimated himself; colleagues thought he was arrogant and they did not really get on well together. Fortunately he left of his own accord. He seems to have a good job now somewhere in a private company. Most probably that suited him more.

D&I: An Opinion or a Knowledgeable Approach?

Organizations who already explored the field of D&I know that the secret of success is not in a scattershot approach or in the simple application of positive action. In congresses about diversity in business, panel discussions all too often end up in political or social discussions rather than dealing with the concrete challenges for organizations. Having the 'right' opinion keeps participants more busy than tailor-made solutions for daily practices. However, an opinion is certainly not enough to gain diversity results. Diversity management keeps coming back on the organizational agenda. Every time, managers think they get rid of it and decide that it is no priority for them or that the efforts will not meet with the results, it re-emerges all the same.

> *But well, now D&I has come back at the agenda. Because new policies want to strengthen the link between urban and rural areas. This demands contacts between farmers and horticulturists on the one side and the diversity of citizens on the other side, including many especially young people with an ethnic minority background that are hardly seen on the agricultural and horticultural schools yet. Peter finds this an interesting idea. Moreover, age has become an issue. In the years to come, the majority of the employees in his department will retire but young employees do not stay long at the ministry; so how to proceed for knowledge preservation?*

You Decide the Best Approach for D&I!

Especially organizations who already have some D&I experience increasingly change their focus from a social to a business approach (read more about this under factor 1). An idealistic conviction is not enough to gain results; the business case must be paramount. The methodology of ten critical success factors6 allows you to apply D&I as integral part of your core business. This methodology is about how and not about what and offers you lessons from theory and practice, many examples and a roadmap to effective D&I.

> *Peter really likes this approach: that he can consider himself, together with his team, what it is that they would like to achieve in D&I.*

---

[6] These principles have been worked out gradually by Seba culture management as a D&I specialist in training, consultancy and projects. Experience shows that organisations make different choices in working on success factors, with results that matter for their particular business.

D&I: Utilize All Talents Available

As described in the case about Cologne, critical situations are the testing moments that prove whether the organization has diverse talents among the staff (read: diverse qualities, antennas, points of view, behavior) and if so, whether their talents are actually utilized for the core business of the organization (inclusion). Is one of the results of the inclusive leadership that the leader and his or her surroundings are facilitated themselves for the major D&I issues of these times?

The word *diversity* is not just about a beforehand, specifically-determined social type but about all the personnel. Indeed, everybody has an identity, a culture and talents to contribute: white men as well as black women, young heterosexuals as well as older homosexuals and so on. D&I do not focus on who or what is different, but on the quality of organizations to gain the best results right in the middle of an ambiguous context of differences.

> *Peter and his department had a long discussion about this. Peter thought: that Moroccan employee we had, would have been a great match for the issue of urban and rural cooperation. He knew the Moroccan communities quite well. Suddenly Peter regrets that the man took another job, because he sees that the field of gay farmers is in good hands with a gay colleague. Still a few colleagues think that nowadays every employee should have the competences to work in policies concerning cities and rural areas, including the many different social groups that live there. They think it should not be attributed to an employee who happens to be gay or a member of an ethnic minority himself. Well yeah, there was not a clear outcome of that discussion. Nevertheless, all admitted that they knew the rural areas very well but that they could not easily make the connection with urban life and certainly not with ethnic minority groups for agricultural and horticultural policies.*

The utilization of all different talents in the organization is not a neutral process. Too many organizations still adhere to that premise. In practice, some talents appear to be utilized more than others. The underutilization of talent happens more frequently when a person's appearance is different. The more visible the difference is, the more people are inclined to react to it with perceptions they have about a certain social group notwithstanding this person's own perception whether he or she belongs to that group and what the nature of that group is (see also under factor 5).

TEN CRITICAL SUCCESS FACTORS

Conscious attention for the presence of diversity among the workforce makes the difference between good and bad performance of culturally or otherwise diverse teams. Studies have also shown that organizations with a scattershot approach, the so-called unmanaged diversity, experience rather the negative effects of diversity: more conflicts and undesirable group formation, more turnover of personnel and an organizational culture where few feel at ease. The benefits occur when the negative effects are consciously counteracted by the management and the organization focuses on clearly described aims for those benefits: the so called managed diversity. The ten critical success factors offer the guidelines for it.

Critical Success Factors for the Optimal Utilization of All Diverse Talents

Vision and change management

1. A clear vision regarding D&I in relation to the organization's overall vision, both economic and social.

2. The existence of or steering toward an organizational culture open to change, to diverse behavior and ways of thinking.

3. Ability to demonstrate the added value of D&I to customers and other stakeholders.

4. Broad support and commitment from the board and management, ensuring benefit and need are recognized throughout the whole organization.

The human factor in the organization

5. All the personnel have motivation, knowledge, and skills to handle differences.

6. Managers who recognize and identify the dynamics of diversity and take action based on the benefits of diversity.

7. Insight into the competences of all personnel in relation to competences relevant to the organization.

Instruments and systems

8. Consolidate D&I principles in systems and instruments for strategic personnel policy, communication policy, marketing policy and management style.

9. Sufficient diversity at all levels of the organization.

10. Board and management are evaluated on the basis of actions and behavior concerning D&I.

The order of the factors does not represent priorities; priorities are set by the organizations themselves. There is a subdivision in organizational themes. The first four factors belong to vision and change management. The next three factors consider the human factor in the organization. The last factors involve conditions and systems. One factor can be more important for an organization than the other, but none can be overlooked.

The great advantage of this concrete list of ten critical success factors is that managers who want to start a D&I initiative can see at a glance what factors play a role in that and what accents or focus they can stress on. It works as an excellent tool to determine where they are now and where they want to go. They look before they leap and can choose those factors that are most critical for their particular business. For example, if they want to start working on the numbers of factor 9 because they think that is the most critical factor for the organization or because politicians ask that from the organization, they find out that they better combine it with factor 2: organizational culture to be able to welcome the newcomers and really utilize their talents or factor 5, managers who can create the conditions for diverse teams to be successful. Like this the chances of success of D&I initiatives become much better.

For Peter, it was clear right away that factor 9 forms a must: in the first place from the point of view age, but Peter also understands that he is not leading the most diverse department of the ministry, having 75 percent of white men aged over 50, however diverse they might be. The department needs more women and more employees from different ethnic minorities.

When Peter discussed the ten critical success factors with his team, the majority thought that the organization should offer more vision, thus factor 1. Also, they missed broad support and commitment from the management, factor 4. Peter felt irritated. This is how things take ages to be realized! He does not want to wait for the higher management. In everyday life, he already sees a lot of diversity, so he would like to choose factor 3 and open the shutters of the department widely for the outside world, or factor 5 where his own employees require more competences to deal effectively with differences.

Valuing and Prioritizing the Critical Success Factors

The analysis to make choices and set priorities for the organization requires discussion. The method of the ten critical success factors supports teams in a thorough approach. A starting-point based on a shared analysis in the organization considerably improves chances of success. Moreover, it can be an eye-opener to hear how colleagues in different parts of the organization feel about the state of affairs regarding D&I. Experience shows that this may vary widely. Before defining what the right steps to take should be, it is important to find out together why the analyses are different.

It was funny when Peter proposed factor 5: motivation, knowledge and skills of the employees to handle differences. Thomas reproached Lars for ignorance about Eid al Fitr (the Feast at the end of Ramadan) but it appeared that Lars has a son-in-law with Iranian roots and he came up with many questions to Thomas that Thomas could not answer. As a result, there was a good dialogue about the competences needed in the department to face the increasing diversity or the desired diversity in agriculture and horticulture. Opinions differed about the existing level of diversity competence among colleagues: Lars might be an expert in the field of Islam, but does that make him the perfect professional to make policies for the connection of urban and rural areas? Thomas is a good communicator but is he also a good communicator when talking to gay farmers? Suddenly Thomas was given the feedback that he makes too many jokes about gays and then the atmosphere was less fun. Thomas asked why they never told him that before. The conclusion was that the team had some kind of taboo to talk about sensitive issues like that and that there was room for improvement for the diversity competences, something to be worked out.

Valuing

To get a general survey of the state of affairs in your own organization a simple and rapid method is to sit down with the management team and other key note players and determine together how you value the organization in the light of D&I. Of course, you can also ask individual departments to do so and compare their results with the results of the executive board.

First, have an individual look at each of the ten critical success factors and define to what extent this factor is ensured in the organization. Let everyone value the success factors by giving it a figure from 1-10: for example, a 4 when it is not very present or an 8 when things go quite well. Then compare the figures in the group. Where is the evaluation similar, where is it different and why is that? The exchange of evaluations lays the basis for a common vocabulary for (analyzing) D&I and a good survey of the strengths and weaknesses of the organization concerning D&I.

Critical Success Factors for the optimal utilization of all diverse talents	
Critical success factors:	Figure 1 - 10
1. A clear vision regarding D&I in relation to the organization's overall vision, both economical and social.	
2. The existence of or steering towards an organizational culture open to change, to diverse behavior and ways of thinking.	
3. Ability to demonstrate the added value of D&I to customers and other stakeholders.	
4. Broad support and commitment from the board and management, ensuring benefit and need are recognized throughout the whole organization	
5. All the personnel have motivation, knowledge and skills in handling differences.	
6. Managers who recognize and identify the dynamics of diversity, and take action based on the benefits of diversity.	
7. Insight into the competences of all personnel in relation to competences relevant to the organization.	
8. Consolidate D&I-principles in strategic personnel policy, communication policy, marketing policy and management style.	
9. Sufficient diversity at all levels of the organization.	
10. Board and management are evaluated on the basis of actions and behavior concerning D&I.	

If you are really in for a challenge, then follow the same process with a group of customers or stakeholders. My experience is that this results in a less positive survey than the one given by the members of the organization itself. However, the reverse can also happen: customers and other relations appear to value the organization quite high on a certain factor. Again, it is important to find and analyze differences: why is the evaluation higher or lower, and what do similarities and differences in evaluation mean for our organization?

This makes Peter enthusiastic, the idea that every colleague will invite one or two people from the agriculture and horticulture field that he is regularly in touch with and that they will do this exercise all together. In his department, the overall enthusiasm lacks but Peter gives them time to consider it and will come back to it later. He knows his team quite well; they are a bit worried that the people from the field will criticize them. However, if he designs the meeting in such a way that it will be about the challenges of the future and that tendencies to blame will be avoided, it is going to be an engaging and interesting experience for the department.

Prioritise

Once figures have been given to the ten critical success factors, the real work begins: how do you and your staff weigh the importance of the various success factors for your own organization, for the personnel, the customers, and the long term? You need to weigh the factors to determine what your next steps should be, because you can't do everything at a time. Management means setting priorities. Making choices is wise but not simple.

The critical success factors, as such, have no order of priority, other than what every organization evaluates and weighs for itself. There is no objective measuring tool that can show you where to start. Defining what success factor is most critical for your organization is and will stay a decision based on your views of the surroundings, the business goals, the market and the existing organizational development.

Working with the Critical Success Factors: The (Im)possibilities

As said before, the method of the critical success factors offers support analyzing the state of affairs in the organization, in setting priorities and shaping a consistent and structured approach.

The Possibilities

It is a method that takes into account your ever-existing lack of time. A quick overview can be obtained of the most important themes that are at stake for your organization and the considerations for priorities and choices to make. 'Look before you leap' is a good and useful maxim also for D&I. Moreover, you can let your managers themselves determine completely or partly what would be the most effective actions without asking days of preparation from them. The critical success factors enable them to develop a tailor-made approach and apply specific local accents (even at department or team level) within a clearly defined framework.

It is one year later. Peter and his team have made their choices. They have agreed on factor 3, the added value of D&I to customers and other stakeholders. Peter is very happy about that. Peter still considers factor 5, motivation, knowledge and skills of the employees to handle differences, as very important but it made his colleagues uncertain at least that is Peter's interpretation so they have postponed that choice. They all agreed upon factor 2, the culture of the organization. First, everybody looked at Peter. Wasn't he the leader and as such responsible for a good culture? So, at that point Peter engaged a good trainer and that worked out well. Now everybody knows that he has a personal contribution to make to realize the desired culture. Other departments in Peter's directorate have made other choices. At least half of those departments are working out a vision (factor 1) and a number of managers decided to follow a course to manage diversity more inclusively in daily practice (factor 6). Peter is still lobbying to convince more managers to apply factor 3, the added value for customers and other stakeholders because he finds the relation with the outside world essential for the ministry they work in.

The Impossibilities

The methodology of the critical success factors does not offer a standard framework for goals and approaches. Neither does it offer a benchmark with other organizations and it does not presume objectivity. On the contrary: our experience is that organizations who have given a score from 1 to 10 to the various factors in one year, might give themselves lower marks in the next year after efforts made to improve D&I. This is not because the organization has not developed positively on the road of D&I but because of the old Greek adage that applies here: 'the more you know, the more you know what you do not know.' So it can happen that in the first year, a manager thinks the diversity competences of his team members are good and scores 8 for factor 5. But after a year of training, recruitment of new employees and discussions with customer panels his views have become more knowledgeable or critical and his score for factor 5 is now 6, although objectively, his employees have further developed their diversity competences. Besides, employees in one organization can be merely positive while in another organization they are mainly perfectionist. For the same level of quality, one organization would give an 8 while the other gives only a 6.

In the beginning, there was competition between departments. Because some gave themselves an 8 for organizational culture (factor 2) mind you, in those departments the staff turnover was the highest, where others only scored a 6. There were managers with a total lack of knowledge about D&I who gave themselves a 7 for support and commitment (factor 4) and even an 8 for taking action based on the advantages of diversity (factor 6); is that a lack of self-awareness or a lack of self-knowledge? But after a while, the importance attached to the scores was reduced and a real dialogue started about what D&I requires from the organization and what elements should be considered first. Peter hopes that he can finally bring in factor 3 as a result of this dialogue because external added value is vital for the work of every ministry.

Therefore, the methodology is not designed to measure objectively, but to give direction and consistency to decision making and implementation concerning D&I. Even though an objective benchmark is impossible, it is possible to compare. Working with the critical success factors gives a framework and a terminology that facilitates the dialogue between very different departments and organizations. It allows for exchange about the perception of chances and the weighting of priorities.

Why should a leader know about all this management stuff?

In the next paragraphs, I describe the critical success factors one by one. At the beginning of this chapter, I told you: leaders do not need to manage all this themselves but leaders must know what is at stake and what the strategy and the choices can be. They must be involved in the evaluation of what is going to work (or not) for the organization and they have to facilitate the people who will engage in the process with sufficient time and resources. This is how giving direction, showing exemplary behavior and organizing mutually reinforce each other so that even in a context of uncertainties, dilemmas and paradoxes you utilize the advantages of diversity for your organization. If you lead an organization where managers know already a lot about D&I, of course you can give more free rein for the management side of inclusive leadership. However, reality teaches us that this is still rarely the case and that inclusive leadership is essential also for the organizational aspects of D&I.

> At the police force, we see that they try to recruit agents for the street who look like the people that are met with in the street. Although the police force has more diversity than jurisdiction has, comparatively that is not enough yet. There are quite some stories of agents with a different background within the police force about the problems they face (internally): nasty manners, jokes and certain comments. Judges only face this in court; the police however face this in the street and in people's homes so they are forced to think about it. Many district chefs are aware of this but they find it difficult to come up with a good approach. It requires a change of culture.
>
> Willem Korthals Altes, senior judge Court of Amsterdam and chair complaints committee National Police

CRITICAL SUCCESS FACTOR 1

*A clear vision regarding D&I in relation to the organization's overall vision,
both economic and social.*

D&I looks like football/soccer, I often noticed. Everybody has an opinion about it, and you will meet all these opinions when you start implementing D&I. Alas, most opinions are not at all based on any scientific evidence or on a business perspective. If you want to implement D&I in your organization, make sure that your management has more than just their own opinion. Such opinions are usually not more sophisticated than:

- I don't mind whether a person is green, yellow, black or blue.

- It shouldn't make a difference.

- All that matters is quality.

- It will all be sorted out in due course.

Research has shown that it is not sorted out in due course, because there are mechanisms in organizations that prevent that. It is, of course, nice when managers state that for them personally it makes no difference whether a person is green or yellow, however it is not enough. Likewise, it is nice when managers think it shouldn't make a difference, but that is an ideal that will not implement itself. People have perceptions, for example, the perception what quality looks like, and those perceptions prevent them from assessing objectively, in spite of their good intentions. Therefore, make sure there is a clear vision that transcends all private opinions of your managers and unequivocally shows the way in relation to the company goals. D&I is a matter of patience and perseverance, and moreover, it demands a certain investment. It is likely that the subject disappears from the agenda gradually and unwittingly or that it is overshadowed by other priorities. Make sure to provide for a clear wording of the necessity of D&I for your organization. What business interests are at stake?

Historically, we can roughly determine two distinctive trends in the approach of D&I. One trend is about business interests and the so-called business case. It is the trend that my consulting company follows and thus the trend that this book belongs to. The other trend is mainly about justice. Following this trend leads to a different effect. So, it is good to make yourself acquainted with the consequences of both visions. The main distinctions between both trends can be described as follows.

Trend A: The Business Case

Working with a business case means putting business interests and opportunities that D&I offers first and foremost. In the trend of the business case the assumption is that companies are well-intentioned and can be convinced to work on D&I by business arguments. D&I is mainly seen as a practical issue: how can a company survive best in a world becoming increasingly diverse, and eventually even be stronger than other companies because of a cleverly applied D&I policy?

Geographically, this trend finds its roots in the United States, by the mouth of professor Thomas Roosevelt, Jr. in the nineties, but the development of D&I as a business case in organizations is limited by the other trend in the United States that represents justice. When projects are started, lots of time is spent discussing the 'right' view on D&I. It often happens that managers and employees start to judge each other morally. It goes without saying that this is not beneficial for the implementation of D&I in daily practices.

In non-Western countries, the business case is more elaborated because their companies are more result-oriented for D&I. Their guideline is not what should be done, but what will have results, and the orientation on aims in the future is stronger than orientation on injustice in the past.

The position of women and employees from different ethnic minorities gets special attention in the business case trend, as well as other more or less visible human characteristics: people with a disability, different sexual orientations, diverse ages, religions, castes, educational backgrounds, with high IQ, different learning styles and lifestyles. The key issue is to learn organizations how to deal with differences and how to use them for the business results. In this perspective, individuals are more central than groups: indeed, no two women are alike, migrants are not all the same, nor are white men. Getting the best out of employees is not possible by approaching them as a group on the grounds of similar appearances or (supposed) common characteristics. This trend pays attention to specific exclusion mechanisms towards certain social groups in organizations. The development of organizations lags behind the diversity in their surroundings. Organizations are not capable to use all the talent available because they cannot recognize it. They overlook opportunities because their sight is too limited for the increasingly diverse reality.

Multiple strategic arguments and a variety of business perspectives can be found for D&I. Your business case can be more on the P-side of your organization or department—for example, the labor market or personnel management—but can also be related to your customers or the complexity of your services and products:

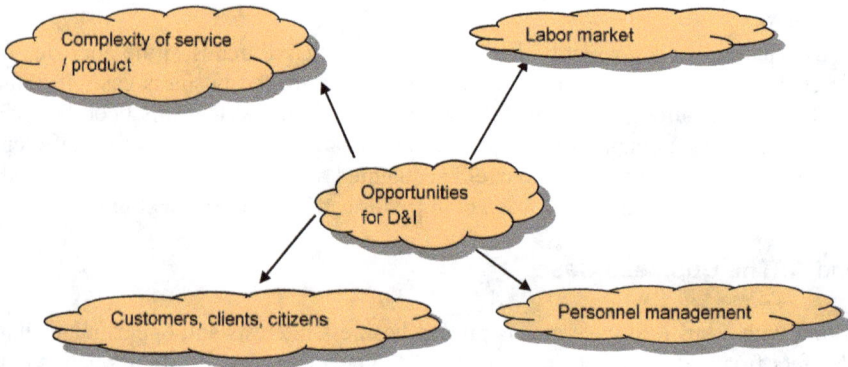

I know a high school with a vice principal of a different ethnic background who has a completely different leadership style. My first thought was: how can the Board deal with that. And in the meantime, the whole culture of that school is filled with pride, of their internationality, of their innovative approaches, of so much. The whole world is in there; that is really very difficult, they have guts. This school will produce our new leaders. These are contexts that give me hope. One way they have to express inclusion is to teach students how to network with companies. Part of the student population completely lacks those skills but because the school is organizing it, they learn how to do it and get access. It was great when I heard a student say: "Now when I am on the tram, I just dare to ask to someone 'and what do you do,' before I wouldn't."

Marij Urlings, director Domain Education & Innovation, Inholland University of Applied Sciences

Working on the business case means that D&I is integrated in the goals and strategy of your company, and in the competences of managers and employees. Personnel policy is important, as well as marketing. Training programs mainly follow these themes and must lead to ideas and actions for daily work. Justice is only partially linked with the business case. Not the whole societal reality of justice and injustice is taken into account, but internal fairness in relation to the assessment of performance and the criteria for promotion is. A study of Deloitte, for example, has shown that in companies that developed an inclusive talent management system, 94 percent has the feeling to be assessed in a fair way, whereas in organizations with only basic systems, this percentage is 35 percent. That is a huge difference and undoubtedly impacts the energy, the enthusiasm, the engagement, and the performance at work.

Context of ambiguities, uncertainties and paradoxes

In the trend of the business case, the interest of the organization is more at stake than the interest of social groups in society. As a consequence, it can be seen as commercial egotism. The assumption then is that a company would not take on social responsibility when it is not a business interest to employ people with a disability or to offer training to employees of 55 years and older. People who think in terms of justice (trend B) can feel a profound mistrust of the 'good intentions' of organizations, and they easily express this distrust in the media. If you follow the trend of the business case for D&I in your organization, this will be your biggest dilemma.

Trend B: Justice

Putting justice first means that social inequality and discrimination are emphasized in D&I policies. In this trend, the main focus is on the position of women and members of ethnic minorities (or 'people of color,' 'Latinos,' and the like) and in recent years increasingly also LGBTQ's. The starting point is that the actual top of organizations, usually consisting of white men, holds and will hold the power positions. So, an important aim to be pursued is sharing of power. In this trend, numbers are important criteria: the results of companies who make an effort for D&I will be measured by the number of women and members of ethnic minorities that these companies employ, also in the top positions. Moreover, these companies must provide safety to workers from these social groups and LGBTQ's: the workplace should be free of mobbing, intimidation and discrimination.

In this trend, it is very important to integrate D&I at the level of the core-values of the organization, and also in personnel policy. In trainings effort are made to convince the participants and make them accept the right analysis of reality, in general this is called raising awareness. Employees need to know what social inequality is, how it feels, and how it works out within and outside of the organization in terms of discrimination and intimidation. The assumption is that when people know that, they will behave better at work. An example of this approach is the training *Brown eyes, blue eyes* that came up in the 90s, lead to quite some comments in the media and seems to live a comeback now. In this training, the participants are divided in groups according to the color of their eyes, brown or blue. These groups are subsequently treated in a different way in terms of power, participation, rules and social behavior. The participants with brown eyes experience how it is to have the say based on the color of their eyes, while the participants with blue eyes experience what it means to be set apart. The shock of this experience is supposed to move participants to behave in a different, better way in the future and to say farewell to discrimination and racism. The underlying vision is that the core problem in organizations is a lack of justice. However, the risk of lasting damage in your company after the use of this method is significant.

A 'softer' training method that is used a lot in relation to what is called 'gender diversity' is the division of management groups in groups of men and groups of women. They get an assignment and the way they deal with the assignment is used as a proof that there are real differences between male and female leadership or management. Then there is a discussion about the fact that female approaches and working ways are less appreciated than the male ones, and why that is the case. Participants experience this often as an eye-opener, however in the meantime their gut feeling can be uneasy about it. That is because the method perpetuates (supposed, earlier assumed) differences rather than creating room for difference regardless the sex of the participant.

Context of ambiguities, uncertainties and paradoxes

In the trend of justice, there is more attention for groups than individuals. Indeed, the differences in the balance of power that exists in society have a knock-on effect in organizations. This is how a part of the societal complexity and politics enter into your organization. Colleagues who do not share the 'intended' conviction can show heavy opposition. Mutual judging can create (new) blockades and frustrations. If you follow the trend of justice for D&I in your organization, this will be your biggest dilemma.

CRITICAL SUCCESS FACTOR 2

The existence of or the ability to steer towards an organizational culture characterized by a willingness to change and open-mindedness to diverse behavior and ways of thinking.

Organizational culture defines implicitly or explicitly the rules of the game in your organization and is an important condition to utilize diversity and create inclusion. Organizational culture can also be lubricating oil: that is why the machine runs smoothly. Everybody knows what is normal, and mutual expectations become predictable. A short, practical definition of organizational culture is the way we do things here (by Deal & Kennedy). A culture that upholds "the way we do things" is inclined to disregard diversity in the organization; different ways of thinking and acting lead to distortion of the status quo and are therefore undesirable.

Newcomers in an organization see themselves confronted with the task to find out quickly about the informal rules and live with them. An employee who is unable to find out the way we do things here becomes an underachiever. Then he or she feels unhappy in the organization because most people like to do things right and have them under control. Probably the organization is also unhappy with the newcomer and sends him or her out again. It is obvious that diversity can foster resistance, be ignored and turn out to be a failure for the organization and the employees involved. Inclusion sounds very nice but an inclusive culture does not come about by itself.

No company can consider organizational culture as an unconscious process. The great variety of backgrounds of employees and customers forces the organization to reflect about its culture and choose and elaborate an identity that is favorable for inclusion. What is the exact meaning of 'open-mindedness to diverse behavior and ways of thinking'? Does that mean that everything is permitted and nobody needs to adapt anymore? Should 'they' not share 'our' values and norms? Just like other issues described in this book, such a debate can quickly become highly emotional and political. The art of inclusive leadership is to encourage a respectful dialogue in the light of the business you're in.

> Open-mindedness to diverse behavior and ways of thinking is the core, you have to open up, and that goes for jurisdiction as well as the police. In the street, my consideration is: is this something that harms a person or is it a different environment and lifestyle. The world is so much more diverse than let us say 50 years ago. For me the limit is to harm others.
>
> Willem Korthals Altes, senior judge Court of Amsterdam and chair complaints committee National Police

Why do some talents find the opportunity to develop further and other talents don't? That is not a standard but a dynamic process, as the theory of perceptions and tokenism shows. In that sense, culture is the most intangible of the ten critical success factors and in the meantime far-reaching.

Perceptions

Perceptions have a major influence on the level of inclusiveness of a culture. Every leader, manager and employee has certain perceptions about people and qualities. Those perceptions derive from education and experience and are also fueled by the (work) environment and the media. For example, perceptions in society about someone's identity and role can drive much of the performance at work. Research has shown that former Yugoslavs in the Netherlands had much more trouble finding a job in the 90s than in the decades before. This could only be explained by the images of war that entered the homes of managers and recruiters every day during several years. It influenced their perceptions and thus the careers of former Yugoslavs, also of those who had already lived in the Netherlands since the 70s.

You cannot keep the thoughts and behavior of your employees from having biases; so, do not turn this into a matter of 'guilt and apology,' that will lead to nothing for nobody. However, for the right approach of D&I, it is a matter that deserves your attention and demands constant scrutiny. Employees who are unwilling to be self-critical and learn frustrate every D&I ambition you have.

Tokenism

An important theory in this respect is the theory of tokenism by Rosabeth Moss Kanter. A token is someone who exemplifies a social group that others perceive as a special category, and not as an individual; the 'one stands for all' principle. That can happen when a single person, for example an Iranian, works among a group of Italians. The token seems to challenge the existing culture by being 'different.' This mechanism causes that only supertokens can be effective: most tokens will just remain underachievers.

Tokenism showed for the first time the significance of numbers and proportion for behavior in organizations: how many persons of a social type work with how many persons of another social type. As proportions begin to shift, so do social experiences. Therefore, to create an effective team in a world of diversity, a numerical tilt must be considered for the organization. This principle is shown in Moss Kanter's figure below:

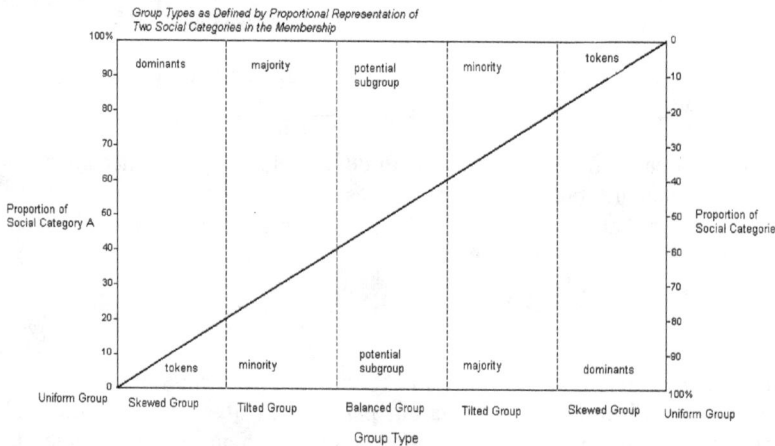

Group Types as Defined by Proportional Representation of Two Social Categories in the Membership

As long as a certain social type represents less than 15 percent, they will be in a token position in relation to the numerically dominant types.

At 15 percent to 35 percent, there is a minority versus a majority. Now the members of a minority group are less seen as a token and more as an individual, although they are still different from the members of the majority group.

The critical border to actually get influence as a social type lies at 30-35 percent. Balance in influence, culture and interaction occurs when the verge of 40 percent is passed. So, the power of the number is strong and will be one of the factors to determine who actually come through in the organization. Quantitative objectives for boards in companies as set by the EU (40 percent), the Netherlands (30 percent) and many other European countries are based on Moss Kanter's findings. It gives inclusive leaders evidence based arguments for initiatives concerning the proportion of numbers in the organization (factor 9).

The theory of Moss Kanter was developed in the 70s of the last century but is still rock solid when dealing with minorities and majorities in teams, is also my experience. The fact that the shift of proportions (partially) determines the social experiences is usually well-received by participants in trainings. They see it as an eye-opener and feel it as a relief: indeed, it is not about their personal lack of virtue, but about the dynamics all team members are part of. And they can all do something about it. Moss Kanter mentions three levels of action for these dynamics:

1. Structuring opportunities.

2. Structuring power.

3. Structuring numbers.

In practice, most organizational efforts concern level 3, the numbers (factor 9). However, for an inclusive culture, the other two levels that lie in the field of the factors 2, 6, 7 and 8 are equally important.

Context of Ambiguities, Uncertainties and Paradoxes

A remark from my side about the theory of tokenism of Moss Kanter is that we are now heading for a workplace without a clearly defined majority and minority for example based upon ethnicity or gender but with a lot of variety in diversity aspects all together. I dare predict that this will lead to similar patterns and mechanisms, be it along more ambiguous lines. There will be more implicitly perceived minorities and majorities that sometimes overlap perceived social groups whereby members of majority for example employees with a certain assertive behavior get promoted while the talents of other more empathic or serving employees is hardly noticed or valued. Group dynamics and the way we do things here can be enormous and block the creation of an inclusive culture that is willing to change. Indeed, the fact that the workforce in the 21st century is increasingly diverse does not guarantee that it will all be sorted out in due course. What the exact dynamics will be and what it will ask from inclusive leaders is uncertain.

Neither do measures governments take to improve the diversity in boards and the like offer solutions. Their rules and laws are based on a specific social group: man/woman and disregard other forms of diversity. But you do need these other forms of diversity to be successful in your business. Governments seem to assume that with the application of the 30 or 40 percent norm, the numbers m/w will result all by itself in organizations that work on the other critical success factors necessary to create inclusive organizations. And indeed, in Europe and also other countries worldwide, the number of women on boards is rising. Nevertheless, the focus on numbers only may increase resentment and threatens the long-term impacts of the measures taken. That precisely is a dilemma for you as an inclusive leader.

Besides, there is also the cultural field of tension between permanent employees and the increasing number of self-employed professionals in organizations (see core argument 3 in the introduction). Often, the permanent employees have found their own routine and they are comfortable with it. These employees form the basis and the cultural heart of your organization. They are the ones who have the historical memory, who coach the self-employed temporary colleagues and ensure the good introduction of the new ones. However, with their 'way we do things here,' they can really oppress the diverse self-employed professionals. When it is your objective to recruit more diversity by employing temporary staff in order to respond better to customer demands, you need very good communication to prevent that your employees experience it as a huge paradox.

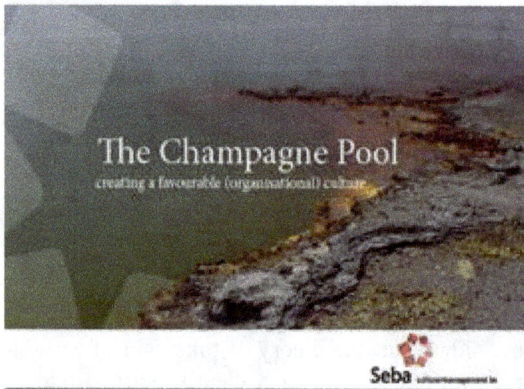

To support you in making your (organizational) culture tangible and adaptable, Seba developed The Champagne Pool: 30 cards with concise theory-cards and many exercises make this card box a ready-for-use tool. It is a good instrument for yourself and others to understand and influence culture.

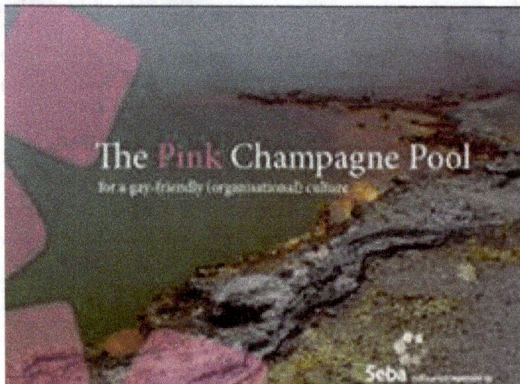

Specifically, for issues concerning sexual diversity Seba made The Pink Champagne Pool. Methodically, it is a toolbox comparable to The Champagne Pool. The relationship between organizational culture and the extent to which LGBTQ colleagues can do their job often remains underexposed. The Pink Champagne Pool deals with the creation of a safe, tolerant culture, raises awareness and enables dialogue in your organization.

CRITICAL SUCCESS FACTOR 3

Ability to demonstrate the added value of D&I to customers and other stakeholders.

Demonstrating the added value of D&I has everything to do with the external profiling of companies, with communication and PR. The biggest challenge is to have a profile consistent with internal reality. A glossy story without basis gives no more than a short term positive effect for your organization and can even work against you in the long term. I showed that in the chapter 'Giving Direction.' Without a clear guiding mix for the decision made by the inclusive leader, the organization cannot succeed in demonstrating the added value of D&I to the outside world. Moreover, for effective communication, a great deal of thought has to go into the Inclusion Framework (p.17): the balance between uniqueness and belonging. I repeat here what that means: an organization that strongly focuses on uniqueness will meet with a lack of cooperation, group thinking and an abundance of stereotypes. But when the accent lies merely on belongingness, there is a risk that certain backgrounds, experiences and opinions are oppressed. Both elements need to be part of your approach of added value to customers and other stakeholders.

On the occasion of an Open Day, the leadership of the University of Applied Sciences of Amsterdam decided to remove their magazine 'Folia' from the shelves because it showed women's bare breasts. With this magazine on the shelves, the university would not offer to the incoming students a 'neutral' context for the choice that 'decides the course of their life,' their choice of a study, the leadership stated. This created a lot of commotion in a liberal city like Amsterdam so a dean of the university was invited in a national talk show to defend their position. However, it was a real struggle for him to explain the decision because the general policy of this university seemed to be the opposite: to acquaint the students with all different influences in Amsterdam. Moreover, he did not want to specify for whom the measure was intended 'because I do not know who will attend at an Open Day.' His opponent, the editor-in-chief of 'Folia' argued that this was part of the nature of Amsterdam and that it was a bad thing to remove that influence from prospective students. Besides he considered this as censorship and said that he would not easily send his child to a university where such things happened. In the debate between the male dean, the male editor-in-chief and the male TV host, the matter that was key question for the female initiators of the discussion about breasts disappeared. Consecutive discussions in the newspaper brought that back to the agenda: why are bare breasts considered as offensive at all? They showed that the debate characterized by sexist clichés, thus playing down the feminist issue. With all this happening, an inclusive image of the university was far away. At the Open Day, itself a campaigning female student distributed the controversial 'Folia' magazines to prospective students—with bare breasts. As a matter of fact, the intended effect of the measure taken was thus undone.

So, the debate did not go very well for the university in the light of the 'ability to demonstrate the added value of D&I towards customers and other stakeholders.' Instead of the image of a liberal, open-minded university, the public profile was created of a university where diversity is a limiting factor. That was probably due to the lack of a guiding mix or to the development of a guiding mix that proved insufficiently consistent in the national debate. Moreover, the university could not make clear how it positioned itself in the balance of the Inclusion Framework.

Of course, D&I also means experimenting and just give it a try. Sometimes that works out well, sometimes it doesn't: trial and error is part of the game. Your organization does not need to have everything in place before being out in public, but it is highly recommended to have a strong awareness of the sensitivities. D&I that is not guided becomes political! The Open Day of the University of Applied Sciences of Amsterdam is another example to prove the evidence of that statement. The university has experience with dozens or even hundreds of open days. In the light of D&I 'neutral' open days no longer exist. The good experiences of the past offer only limited guarantee for the future. Open days that demonstrate the added value of D&I are not obvious but rather a quest that requires a joint effort of all involved in the organization.

What are the 'open days' of your organization? And what people with what qualities for D&I are responsible for them?

> Strictly religious protestant groups have asked Youké for an offer in social services. A discussion arose in the institution, why us, why would a religious organization not do that? But well, they have asked us to do it and that is exciting when thinking on the basis of their own talent and resources. We have for example a program for 'divorce in open conflict.' Their demand, however, is more focused on trying to keep the family together anyway.
>
> Fawzia Nasrullah, CEO youthcare institution Youké

With the right approach of D&I, your products or services will improve for the customer: they will be more tailor-made or the way they are treated is better so customer loyalty improves. If you can really do it, you will have a strategic advantage over your competitors. New customers, new candidates for the job, and a better image are the most important results you can harvest. At the level of the job market an organization where D&I is the norm, has an advantage as people increasingly appreciate to be approached on the basis of uniqueness and qualities rather than on a mall implied by organizations that will make them feel stuck. The same goes for customers. It is no longer feasible to give a central place to the company's own structures and products. It is an easy thing to say, 'the customer comes first'; the challenge in an individualizing and globalizing world is enormous.

The strategic advantage goes, of course, on condition that the public knows you are doing this. The world is too complex to think that people will notice all by themselves. D&I offers specific opportunities because a number of activities has occurred around this theme. More and more countries have charters that can be signed by profit and not-for-profit organizations, promising that they will work on gender diversity or cultural diversity or all diversity. It is a great opportunity to create new networks and exchange experiences. You can join those activities or even create activities yourself and thus demonstrate the added value of D&I for your customers and other stakeholders.

The demonstration of the added value of D&I has a strong influence on D&I practices in your organization. Indeed, when cleverly applied there will be more customers with diverse demands. This shows to your managers and employees that they really have work on D&I, it is motivating, they know why they do it. From that point of view, the impact of this critical success factor is great. It is as if D&I is implemented from outside in.

> Sometimes the arrogance of the Dutch entrepreneurs is enormous. In Russia at an embassy get-together I spoke to a Dutch entrepreneur who gave an example of something Turkish entrepreneurs are really good at. There was a big project in Eastern Russia to build half a town. A Turkish and a Dutch CEO were asked to go there to do business. The Dutch CEO finally decided not to go because there was no five-star hotel. The Turkish CEO however did go and slept three days on a mattress on the floor. The Russians respected that so much that he got the contract. Dutch people think too often within the limits of their comfort zone and cannot do business in a different way.
>
> Atilla Aytekin, CEO Orange Games

The reflections to demonstrate the added value of D&I in combination with the learning process through dialogue with your diverse environment bring your organization almost automatically to a point of no return. At that point, there is little time to dwell any longer at the question 'why' and you can start to work on the 'how.' That supports in the meantime the creation of an organizational culture favorable for D&I, as described under factor 2. You open the doors widely to the outside world and you will notice that also the organizational culture wins with that!

Finally, four examples of companies who have been working on D&I since many years. They speak with authority because their policies and actions are consistent. They are rightly proud to demonstrate the added value to customers and stakeholders. Leiden University presents the goals for D&I in relation to talent development:

> *Everyone, whether a student or a member of staff, should feel welcome and supported, as a member of the academic community, but also as a person, with all his or her unique characteristics and experiences. Only then can everyone fulfil his or her full potential.*

> *There are many ways in which our university community is diverse: we differ from one another in ethnicity, gender, sexual orientation, health, religion, age, socio-economic background, and in many other respects. To allow this diversity to flourish, our university has to be truly inclusive.*

> *The globalisation of education and the increasing diversity of Dutch society offer opportunities for developing talent and giving an impetus to innovation and creativity. But how do we do that? It imposes new demands of the support and guidance of students, PhD candidates and staff. It requires us to create equal opportunities, irrespective of sex, cultural background, sexual orientation or physical limitations, so that talent can flourish fully. For these ideals to be achieved, there has to be a climate in which everyone feels at home, is accepted as they are, and identifies with the university's values. We haven't reached that stage yet, but colleagues commit every day to bringing closer the ideals of diversity, equal opportunities and inclusiveness.*

Valid Express, a courier service, has reversed the perspective since many years, to see what employees can do:

> *At Valid Express, we always look at the work someone can do instead of focusing on a physical disability or chronic illness. We find it more important that a courier is enthusiast, accurate and reliable than to focus on a physical impairment. Are you one of those go-getters who is proactive in life and who does not succumb to pessimism? Then working at Valid Express courier services might just be the thing for you.*

PWC connects D&I directly to the services offered:

> *Creating value through diversity. Be yourself. Be different.*

> *Our approach: At PwC, we respect and value differences. We know that when people from different backgrounds and with different points of view work together, we create the most value for our clients, our people and society.*

Sodexo, winner of several awards in D&I, shows that D&I is integrated in their core business:

> *As the leader in Quality of Life services, Sodexo is committed to providing to all employees the best possible work life experience regardless of age, gender, nationality, culture or personal characteristics. That is why we have always positioned diversity and inclusion as the cornerstone of our culture and a fundamental component of our overall growth strategy.*

Context of ambiguities, uncertainties, and paradoxes

Demonstrating the added value of D&I sets high requirements to the ability of inclusive leaders to create a real positive climate and learning organization. As shown in the many examples in this book, mistakes influence the success factor of added value more than the other success factors. As a consequence, there is pressure on the leaders to 'act,' to express strong statements or to take 'substantial measures.'

However, on page 77, Andre Peperkoorn advocates for a new type of strong leader who can deploy vulnerability as strength. Do not pull out at the first setback and certainly do not step into the pitfall of blaming and shaming all kind of individuals, to show through verbal sturdiness that you have it all under control. Cooperate step by step with your employees to improve and innovate your guiding mix and apply the Inclusion Framework.

CRITICAL SUCCESS FACTOR 4

Broad support and commitment from the board and management, ensuring benefit and need are recognized throughout the whole organization.

Finding broad support and commitment for D&I certainly isn't self-evident. The implementation of D&I is a form of change management where you can meet with quite some persistent resistance. Diversity can feel like new shoes with pressure points. Your old shoes are well run-in and fit properly and you get blisters in the new shoes. The problem with diversity is: it forces you to think about yourself. In the confrontation with (assumed) differences, the existing self-evidence seems to disappear. And that is not just tiring; it can even make it impossible to cooperate. It is often an important part of the failure of mergers and acquisitions. A lot is invested in designing and implementing new organizational structures and adjusting financial and ICT systems and little to no attention is given to the human factor in the organization: the employees have to do it automatically, without investments. However not all are happy to receive new shoes, even if they get them for free! People tend to walk on their old shoes as long as possible, even when they start to show visible wear marks. And once the perceptions about 'the other' have developed into fixed images, the us-versus-them way of thinking has arisen, and you will have a lot of trouble introducing your ideas about inclusion in cooperation and communication for the new organization.

Moreover, there are a lot of societal tensions that can be related to certain social groups. Just have a look in today's newspaper: every conflict worldwide seems to have a diversity component. We see terrible incidents concerning the rights of women and LGBTQ-people. We see ethnic conflicts and conflicts between people of different religious denominations. Your employees are informed about them every day in the media and that has a lot of often implicit and deep impact. They are afraid of conflicts, attacks and even war and they are afraid that life the way they can lead it right now will disappear, that their rights will be violated and that their freedom is at stake. This intense reality enters your organization the moment you start to talk about a business case for D&I. It is very possible that by just mentioning the word *diversity*, you evoke completely different images than a business case. That in itself is not right or wrong; it is just the way it is. Be aware of these dynamics; it should make you consider thoroughly how to bring the message across. Inclusive leadership means that the (implicit) fears that people have are included in your explanation about benefit and need. But never allow fear to rule.

Like in all processes of change, finding allies who want to go for D&I with you is of paramount importance. Work with the willing! Look at the managers and also at eventual informal leaders in your organization, and probe your chances. Potential allies can be divided in five categories:

1. The idealists

   These are the people who are in favor of diversity because they adhere to a certain conviction or political vision. Usually, these are people with great perseverance. There is no need to fear that they will easily change their talk and opinion, you can rely on them. A difficult side idealist can have is their normative view of the world; their judgment can discourage others. Also, it is more difficult for them than average to recognize the concrete problems D&I brings. They are inclined to consider them as a sign of resistance or bad intentions, so it can be hard for them to be creative in finding solutions.

2. People who have experienced exclusion themselves

   Whoever has experienced exclusion understands very well that for the utilization of all talents more is needed than just trust that 'we can do it.' These people can mainly be found in categories of people who are different, or being observed as different, by other colleagues at work: women, migrants, ethnic minorities, gays and lesbians, highly intelligent people, people with a handicap, Muslims. Also, people who work as the only elderly between young colleagues or the opposite have this experience, and even people who have been victims of mobs at school or at work. Moreover, it appears that parents from a child adopted from another part of the world start to see the world around them with sharper diversity eyes, as well as fathers whose daughters started a great career to find out around the age of thirty that the glass ceiling still exists.

   The advantage these people offer is that they quickly recognize the exclusion mechanisms in their own organization and can easily put their finger on the sore spot. However, they can be inclined to identify personally with the subject. Their expectations can sometimes be too high. They may suddenly quit because it is all too much for them.

3. People who have experienced D&I in other organizations

   They are not many yet but they do exist: people who, usually with pleasure, worked in an organization that was more diverse and inclusive than yours is. Almost always they have felt it as a step back to find themselves in a more uniform organization again. If you ask them, they say it is 'boring.' When they belong to the dominant social group, they miss the challenge to empathize continuously in others and to show who they are themselves and what they stand for. When they belong to a minority group, they get tired of being again considered as an exception in your organization; because in a diverse organization nobody is the norm so nobody can be treated as an exception.

The people in this category do not necessarily see it as their task to build a D&I friendly organization but when they do they have the right influence. Indeed, they know what they talk about; they have lived the first stages of D&I already. Not only can they reassure colleagues that it is possible to work on D&I without the so often feared 'loss of quality,' but also show how much fun it really is when not every colleague has the same predictability and behavior.

4. People that deal a lot with diversity in practice

    Some managers have a lot of interaction with the outside world by nature of their function. They lead market research and get the results about trends on the labor market or their department has a desk where diverse customers or citizens turn to with different requests. They may have personnel working in the street or at customers' homes where they are confronted with all kinds of diversity. They are guest-speakers at universities where they see the diversity of today's students; they organize customer meetings in diverse areas or receive phone calls from chairs of LGBTQ interest groups, people with disabilities, HIQ's and so on. There is no need to explain to these people the benefit and need of D&I. Moreover, they can reflect quite well on the business case that is at stake for your organization.

5. People who grew up in diversity

    Today's labor market has an increasing group of young people who are very familiar with diversity. The discussion of the baby boom generation about the 'importance' of D&I and the risk that more diversity could mean 'less quality' does not appeal at all to this group. Diversity is simply the starting point for them. They prefer paying attention to inclusion. How do we make sure that we utilize all talents available, how do we create an attractive offer of our diverse customers? What is the secret of inclusion and how can I contribute to it? If your organization has few young colleagues among the management, then try to engage young colleagues in D&I through network meetings because their perspective is the future of this theme in your organization.

> How to get attention for diversity in the organization? In any case through incidents. For example, there was a lot of attention in the media for a female employee who converted to Islam and could not continue her job at the Royal Netherlands Marechausse on the basis of a renewed safety screening. This lead to quite some internal dialogue.
>
> When there are no incidents, it is possible to create them. Thus, we had research done at the unit of Mobile Safety Supervision, to find out to what extent our profiles and selection procedures contained discriminatory factors. That process brought about a lot of discussion also with employees of specific ethnic backgrounds. We have for example quite a lot of young employees with Moroccan and Turkish roots and they questioned their colleagues: what perceptions do you have about me then? Indeed, despite all the sensors in cameras there is still always a gut feeling.
>
> We also gave a presentation in the Marra (the highest decision, making body of the Royal Netherlands Marechaussee) after the Seba masterclass D&I, where we asked colleagues to join us in rapping. Questions arose, they felt 'observed.' This is how we created a dialogue about leaving one's comfort zone and the feeling to be observed. Can you imagine that others also felt like that and if you do, will you rationalize until it disappears or accept it?
>
> André Peperkoorn, deputy commander Royal Netherlands Marechaussee

Context of ambiguities, uncertainties and paradoxes

Often the influences from the outside world form the biggest risk for you to work on support and commitment because some people cleverly manage to use news reports for their us-versus-them way of thinking. Suppose you have acquired a company and the media report that it was involved in fraud or the name of the company appears in the Panama Papers as a money channeling party; the us-versus-them way of thinking will be (ab)used to the max by the former opponents of the acquirement. Another example, think of the two female CEO's with Turkish background, having top positions in Dutch organizations. Both had to resign with a lot of commotion and public attention around the case. The Netherlands are not ready yet for Turkish women on top, is what I heard in circles of Turkish-Dutch career women. If they had not been Turkish women, they would have never even got that far, is what I heard among Dutch managers. Now it is your task as an inclusive leader to maintain the right balance between judging what goes wrong and breaking the circle of us-versus-them.

CRITICAL SUCCESS FACTOR 5

All the personnel have motivation, knowledge and skills to handle differences.

'But I meant well' is what we hear people sometimes say in a somewhat offended tone when they made remarks that are considered as discriminatory or sexist by others. Many people mean well but good intentions alone are not enough. If you make a mistake in bookkeeping, you can't get away with good intentions either. It is nice that you have them, but the necessary competences matter too. The inclusive leader asks more from his employees than just good intentions and focuses on learning and improving; just like this goes for other issues in the organization. And yes, mistakes can and will be made. An employee can make a discriminating or sexist remark, but not repeatedly: everybody needs to face their own attitude and practices, to acknowledge mistakes and to cooperate on the road to more inclusion. A bit less moral indignation on the one side and a bit more openness and thorough commitment on the other side will actually help inclusion move forward.

> Dialogue is very important. Experience has shown that there is more scope for discussing action perspectives and (im)proper treatment in the operations of Royal Netherlands Marechaussee than in the internal relationships. Between colleagues these are difficult discussions because the usual distance to the 'person concerned' is lacking in the collegial, almost family-like structure of the Royal Netherlands Marechaussee.
>
> André Peperkoorn, deputy commander Royal Netherlands Marechaussee

Competence is needed because with the increasing amount of differences or increasing awareness of differences, implicit conscience and implicit experience are no longer adequate. Diversity should no longer be something that 'happens' to us and appears as a coincidence. It must become an instrument that we can proactively apply in order to create more inclusive practices.

A scientist who has given a well thought out and applicable model for intercultural competence is Wasif Shadid. Shadid speaks about 'intercultural' communication and 'intercultural' competence. In the elaboration of his model, he is already very close to diversity in the larger sense of the word as he also considers characteristics as age or socio-economic class as a subculture. He makes clear how things work out when two people meet and experience each other as different. Reciprocal perceptions influence the conversation and thus the success of the intercultural encounter. This is how he developed the notion of intercultural competence that we call in this book diversity competence (this is possible because of the way Shadid himself defined culture).

> As a Hindustani female director, I have for a long time operated in
> tandem with a white male director. How did that go? Well, he was
> always the first to shake hands; he was in the center of the attention and
> the discussion even though I was chair of the direction team. Such things
> need to be talked about on the basis of self-confidence, I had to dare to be
> vulnerable and I also learned to step forward myself.
>
> Fawzia Nasrullah, CEO youthcare institution Youké

How does intercultural contact work?

Shadid remarks that a society consists of many subcultures. Those can be different
political parties or different socio-economical classes or age-groups. Most probably
you recognize the phenomenon that all these subcultures have their own 'language.'
Even families can be characterized by a specific way of communicating.

The term intercultural communication is usually applied to meetings of people
coming from different countries. But that is a relative fact, Shadid says.
Communication is not so much intercultural by one's membership of certain groups,
but mostly by the difference in views that exists within groups about social and
cultural issues. For example, intercultural communication is also strongly present after
merging processes: the members of the two merging organizations each have their
own subculture that becomes manifest when meeting with the merging partner.

It is quite conceivable that differences disappear when two people meet who are
quite different in background. This happens, for example, when both of them appear
to be a fan of the same football club or when they are both interested to set up in
business. The reverse is also possible. Someone expects to find a kindred spirit but
experiences a world of difference during the conversation. So, the intercultural
meeting is not an objective fact, it is highly dependent of the perceptions of the
partners involved: the employees and the customers of your company! Do they
perceive the other as one of their own, or as a token (see also factor 2)?

The reciprocal perceptions are influenced by the subculture of each of the
partners involved. People from a certain culture expect certain things based on the
course of the communication. The more similarities in culture or knowledge of the
partner's culture, the more effective the communication will be. Suppose you work in
an organization that merged half a year ago. Probably you can hear colleagues say
how much easier they communicate with colleagues coming from their 'own'
organization than with colleagues from the 'other' organization. Maybe you will also
hear them complain about differences in views and ways of working. Their 'own'
colleagues only need half a word to understand while the 'other' colleagues often do
not meet their expectations.

Besides subculture, it is also perception that influences communication. People
are inclined to have perceptions to classify the social environment in groups with
specific characteristics (young people, Americans, Asians, the French, women, Arabs,
gays, doctors). Most people see the groups they themselves belong to as more positive
than those they don't belong to. Prejudices about themselves and the other can lead to
stereotyping and when it goes beyond that, to discrimination. A stereotype soon

becomes a self-fulfilling prophecy: in the behavior of the other people they see what they expect based on the prejudice they have. But that is always at least partly incorrect and thus not effective for the communication.

Often, it appears that contact with people who belong to a group with supposed unfavorable characteristics, are avoided as much as possible. For example, after a merger that has not gone well, stereotyping and blaming the other for unfavorable characteristics can become a popular pastime. Employees try to solve the problems at work as much as possible with their 'own people'; they avoid cooperation with employees from the merging partner. Indeed, more than the actual characteristics of the 'other' colleagues, the perceptions and the stereotyping stand in their way.

The intercultural meeting takes place within a context and that context matters. Take, for example, the message: 'Madam, you are completely safe.' For the interpretation of the message by the woman involved, it makes a difference whether these words are spoken at night at a deserted station, in a street full of wild football supporters, in bed at home, or in a queue in front of a counter.

For D&I, experience has shown that impressions from the media offer an unfavorable context for intercultural contacts. For example, after Hurricane Katrina destroyed New Orleans, the media showed black people as people full of violence who were looting the city. Not just the army, but also helpers, were strongly influenced by this perception and that had unfavorable consequences for their actions in the days after the disaster.

There is no escape from the context we live in. Shadid's model makes clear that it is within that specific context that we must learn to shape our successful intercultural contacts. Therefore, we need to have diversity competence.

Diversity Competence

The lucid description of diversity competence that Shadid offers is a great tool for you if you have the ambition to handle differences not as a coincidence but as an instrument for the implementation of D&I. For Shadid, diversity competence consists of three components:

1. Motivation

    First of all, people need to be motivated to have and maintain social relationships with members of different cultural groups. The motivation is especially influenced by:

    - self-confidence: how anxious is a person to make a bad impression or to lose one's own social identity or to be dominated?

    - obviousness about the aim of the meeting

    - the expected reward

- prejudices

- earlier unpleasant experiences with members of the other group

- the distance a person wants to keep towards a specific cultural group

Generally speaking people, experience a large cultural distance towards the other when they expect to have few personal or cultural similarities and when they feel uncertain in the contact. Similarities make people to be attracted to one another ('birds of a feather flock together'). Like that the communication is more smoothly from the beginning, a relationship is built more easily. By lack of cultural similarities, a bridge can be made for example by shared interests, views or lifestyles. That reduces uncertainty and the fear for the unknown that comes with it.

2. Knowledge

When people lack knowledge, the different expectations they have may lead to incorrect interpretations. What one person considers as polite or honest can be considered as humble or impertinent by the other. That is why knowledge is indispensable: about the situation, about the best behavior, about the best way to get information, about differences between people and their social positions. Knowledge of communication rules and verbal and non-verbal codes is essential to make the right predictions and to formulate expectations concerning the best behavior of oneself and of others. Different norms and values for friendship and hospitality can result in different unfavorable interpretation of behavior, for example as unreliable or stingy. Norms for eye contact, interpersonal distance, and physical contact are examples of non-verbal codes that can differ a lot in every culture or social group.

3. Skills

Communication is not just about what is said, but also about how it is said. The variety of how is large: speaking slowly and clearly, supporting the other by nodding, smiling, saying yes and indeed, creating a warm and understanding atmosphere; moreover, empathy and adaptability to consider the wishes of the conversation partner. These skills are not fundamentally different from general communication skills but appear to be more difficult to apply in a diverse context.

Another major skill is the understanding that the other is an individual and not a representative of a certain group. For this self-knowledge is a pre-condition as well as searching for similarities and common characteristics.

Finally, self-disclosure is important: the capacity to give verbal or non-verbal information about oneself to the conversation partner so that mutual involvement and confidence arises. Again, this always goes for communication; yet in an intercultural meeting, this counts more than average because the knowledge about each other's background is at least at the start of the relationship limited.

Context of ambiguities, uncertainties and paradoxes

Your employees may make mistakes and learn from them, but where do you draw the line? Discrimination, for example, is prohibited by law. So, what do you do when your HR director finds (un)conscious discrimination by one of your employees? When that employee gets a notification in his file, the grapes are sour especially when it involved a colleague in the same department. How will those two colleagues continue to cooperate happily ever after? But if you 'let go,' what is the signal you send to that colleague that experienced discrimination and to the rest of them? How do you keep the pressure on to ensure that people are really willing to learn? Think about it also because most people consider themselves as more diversity competent than they are in reality; I can say that after 20 years of work in D&I.

As the wording of Shadid is quite voluminous and abstract, but his theoretical basis is very strong, Seba has developed a practical card game about diversity competence, Makeda. Makeda helps your managers and employees to find out for themselves with each other how they can develop this competence further. What has always been something rather individual and a competence developed 'by accident' is now a professional requirement for all employees.

CRITICAL SUCCESS FACTOR 6

Managers who recognize and identify the dynamics of diversity, and take action based on the benefits of diversity.

Provided that it is well-managed, diversity at work leads to more innovation, creativity and better quality of decision making. Provided that it is well managed. But what exactly does that mean? The word dynamics of diversity was deliberately chosen for this success factor. Because diversity is not a fixed given; it only exists in the light of how we see the other and how the other sees us. Nobody is diverse when he or she is alone! Everybody is normal until someone else joins. That creates certain dynamics and these dynamics determine whether people start to cooperate, whether a salesman can really sell something to a customer, whether a specialist makes the correct diagnosis, whether your team becomes inclusive and so on. The dynamics of diversity demand three things from a manager:

1. Recognizing the dynamics

2. Daring to identify them

3. Taking action based on the benefits of diversity

The simple understanding that there is such a thing as dynamics of diversity often supports managers already to ignore the all-too-often occurring reflex of denial and refusal to take responsibility. For example, forms of dynamics of diversity that we see a lot are the tendencies employees have to categorise each other and/or to form groups along specific social type lines. So, it is not the manager's 'fault' when employees act like that. But it is the manager's responsibility to put these processes on the right track.

To act when stereotyping jokes occur: who have difficulty to do so?

- The manager who likes to be the best man in the room?

- The manager who only assesses performance based on measurable targets?

- The anxious manager: they might as well turn against me?

- The manager who thinks in terms of groups rather than individuals?

- The manager without empathy for 'losers'?

Regularly the dynamics of diversity start with apparently insignificant situations where team members use remarks and so-called jokes to set others apart. Mary Rowe (MIT Boston) called them micro-inequities[7]: an accumulation of small inequalities in daily work. Thus, certain colleagues are hampered to contribute with their full talents and the mutual relationships become hollow.

Some examples:

- Ah, you're free today? (to a parent who leaves earlier than others to pick up a child from the daycare centre)

- By the way how do you manage things for the children? (Question asked to women, not men)

- Stop stop, do not bend in front of my desk. (to a gay man)

- You are late, must be Caribbean time yeah? (in a variety of cultures and countries)

- Yes, this is how we know 'your kind'! (the colleague is not an individual but a representative of a specific group)

It is advisable to handle this kind of situations immediately when they occur at the first remark and not finally after many incidents. In doing so managers do not just prevent that an individual employee will be limited in his or her contribution, they also set the tone for manners and inclusion right from the beginning.

Years later, in 2008, Rowe added the concept of micro-affirmations[8]. She notices that some managers were very capable in managing the most diverse talents. She studies what they did and concluded that it was a sequence of a whole range of small actions managers used to create opportunities and give their personnel the feeling to be a valuable part of the whole (the sense of 'belongingness,' see the Inclusion Framework on page 17). Rowe's concept of micro-affirmations is very similar to more general concepts such as learning organizations and appreciative inquiry. However, she does not assume that they are neutral. Micro-affirmations demand a deliberate reflection on inclusion and exclusion in teams. In fact, they can be targeted actions in the light of D&I. Every manager should be able to apply them:

- Friendly treatment

---

[7] Definitie Rowe, 1973: Micro-inequities is apparently small events which are often ephemeral and hard-to-prove, events which are covert, often unintentional, frequently unrecognized by the perpetrator, which occur wherever people are perceived to be "different."

[8] Micro-affirmations are apparently small acts, which are often ephemeral and hard-to-see, events that are public and private, often unconscious but very effective, which occur wherever people wish to help others to succeed.

- Listening

- Giving credit

- Helping team members to create a favorable network and other opportunities

- Giving honest, specific, timely, consistent and clear feedback that supports team members to build on their strengths and to overcome real (and not just perceived) weaknesses.

Like many other measures that aim to realize inclusion, not just the 'other' team members but all team members profit when the manager applies micro-affirmations. Most people will recognize the uneasy feeling when they got feedback based on certain prejudices or incorrect assumptions. The same goes for the unpleasant experience that some team members are always listened to while others are systematically ignored.

The fact that Rowe added the concept of micro-affirmations to the existing concept of micro-inequities is somehow a symbol of the development of the field of D&I. Diversity sets the focus mainly on the difference and wants to analyze where that derives from and how a person can contribute without giving up one's own unique identity. Inclusion sets the focus mainly on the art of belongingness: which measures are effective to realize that. Nowadays, practical inclusiveness gets much more attention than before.

> Students think much broader than we do; they want a minute's silence for Paris and also for attacks in all the other cities. So, they will not participate in the minute's silence that we organize as their school. A real inclusive leader has guts and tries to find the connection with these students.
>
> Marij Urlings, director Domain Education & Innovation, Inholland University of Applied Sciences

There are roughly five response modes in the confrontation with differences in teams. The first inclination is to follow one's own 'nature,' for example the anxious and uncertain manager we mentioned before would naturally choose for dominance, adaptation or avoidance. The schedule below wakes him up: hey, I got more possibilities.

Five response modes to manage differences

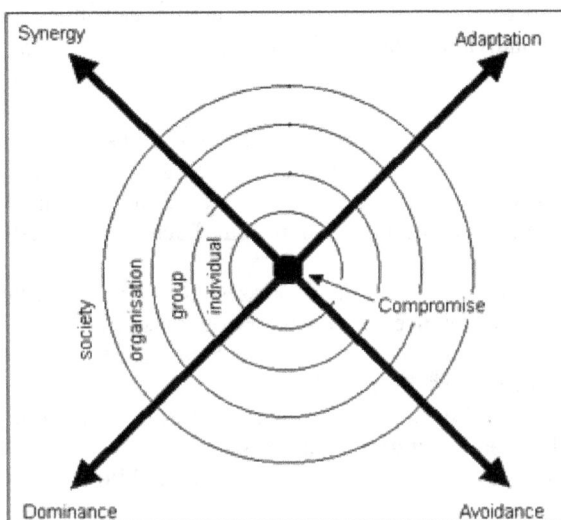

1. Dominance

    I impose my way and I determine how we cooperate and communicate, because my way is the best way.

2. Adaptation

    We have to cooperate and communicate and we have to find a way to do that, so why not do it your way. Or: I am new here so I accept your rules ('when you are in Rome you act like the Romans').

3. Avoidance

    We act as if we don't see or notice (for example because of political correctness, fear of conflict, fear to be accused of discrimination) or: this is not important enough to make trouble about it so just leave it.

4. Compromise

    I will do it a bit my way and you do it a bit your way. This time we follow your rules; next time, our rules. Both of us win some and both of us lose some.

5. Synergy

> Create a new way to approach things that transcends the different ways of the parties or individuals involved, and that utilizes the strong sides they both have.

In daily practice of diverse organizations, I come across many situations where managers wonder: how to deal with this now? Finding the best response mode can be complicated and managers' time is short. Dominance, adaptation and avoidance are the most time-saving responses in the short term. Each of these responses have their own disadvantage.

Through dominance, the manager suppresses the potential conflicts, but he or she leaves no space for differences or creative solutions. Such a response mode is especially useful in times of crisis. In that case, the manager should not live with the illusion that he or she utilizes diverse talents for the organization. All he or she does is prevent harmful effects of diversity on the cost of those who lose out until in a quieter moment the problem can be fundamentally solved.

Through avoidance, the manager leaves it to the field of force in the team to do the job. Whatever the result might be, it is rarely a good cooperation in diversity. Avoidance can serve as a way for a manager to win time for better observations. As long as the manager hasn't spoken out yet, the game will be played in the same way as ever. The manager can quietly consider who is having what position or role in this field of force. But the time must come that the manager turns observations into action. And when remarks are discriminating or intimidating, the manager always has to do something about it immediately because it sets the norm. Avoidance will certainly be interpreted as approval by people who make these kinds of remarks.

Through adaptation, the manager easily becomes part of the problem instead of the manager of it. Another risk is that the manager loses energy to cope with things and finally ends up in a burn-out situation. Adaptation as a response mode has a limited expiration date. In the long term, this manager will lose grip on the team. The dynamics that triumph will then be the dynamics of the survival of the fittest.

Compromise usually shows better results. The different involved parties can keep a part of their identity or working ways. The manager listens carefully. He or she makes sure that what matters to the persons involved is made part of the solution. That is why compromise goes one step further than adaptation.

Synergy is the ideal approach because it does not just involve the uniqueness and interests of all the parties and individuals involved; it also focuses on the utilization of their strengths. This response mode offers the best opportunity to utilize diverse talents for the organization and create inclusive teams. Characteristic of the response mode of synergy is the fact that the manager will reserve his judgement and show respect and listen, also in cases where he doesn't understand quite well what is happening. He dares to mention what he observes and asks questions about how to interpret it. Not listening is the worst thing a manager in a diversity situation can do. Immediately passing one's judgement over the situation, taking action on an ad hoc basis—it is the best way to lose D&I grounds. A manager who wants to apply synergy has to dispose of uncertainty tolerance: he is able to live with the fact that, for the time being, the meaning of a situation or a person's intention stays indistinct.

> For the acquisition of Hello Kids, we kept on travelling to France, we went there five times. No deal was made. It appeared that these meetings were part of the process. The second meeting didn't even discuss the deal at all, only the developments in the sector. In such a situation, I give direction. A manager wants to force the process and pays little or no attention to feelings. The sense of urgency is considered differently in the Netherlands than elsewhere, in the Netherlands people like to have grip when and why a deal is made.
>
> Atilla Aytekin, CEO Orange Games

> Acting in a world of uncertainty: who have difficulty to do so?
>
> - The manager who wants everything to be measurable?
>
> - The perfectionist who cannot make mistakes?
>
> - The decision maker: let me determine that?
>
> - The stereotyper who prefers clearly defined social groups?
>
> - The manager who is afraid that existing norms and values are at stake?
>
> - The control freak that has to know at the beginning how it will end?

My experience is that managers with a good portion of uncertainty tolerance can be very popular among many different people in the organization due to the respect they show.

The relationship is essential; power does not lead to content but to pawns. How can we criticize in such a way that we make progress? That is the climate an inclusive leader will create. Teachers are not natural inclusive leaders. Often, they are focused on their own business, to make it go well. Cooperation between disciplines is very difficult and also in the classroom it does not work out by itself.

Inclusive leadership in the classroom succeeds most of all when teachers have a group during a long time. Inclusion means: the teacher is no longer the boss but a resource in the own responsibility and task of students. Students are mutual sounding boards and they do not consider each other as rivals. They learn because teachers teach and also through mutual feedback. They form a community where the members are willing to help each other and able to show vulnerability. And members who fail to do or contribute anything will drop out.

A vulnerable attitude as teacher is cumbersome. If you show vulnerability in the classroom in the beginning, students will just eat you. When you do it with students who also do it themselves and they respect your role as resource, then the key question of students changes in 'can you help me with this?' instead, of 'what do I have to do?' This is why embodying inclusive leadership requires a process.

Mohamed Aadroun, teacher business administration Amsterdam University of Applied Sciences

Context of Ambiguities, Uncertainties and Paradoxes

When it comes to the dynamics of diversity, managers do not make their presence felt especially when they (unconsciously) fear to be accused themselves of discrimination, sexism and the like. The strange thing is, they might even be right. Because there are leaders and executive directors who refuse to open their ears for problems: whoever reports them, apparently isn't in control and is indeed being blamed for them. Thus, problems continue to proliferate below ground with undesirable outcomes that 'nobody' saw coming. Managers will only take action based on the benefits of diversity if there are inclusive leaders who enable them to do so and do not shun taboos.

You can see it with football trainer Diego Simone (Atletico Madrid): he is involved, runs around, shows empathy, expects intensity and also gives that himself and then his players show that too. When they score, they run to each other, they do it together. Diego is not a 'big boss' but brings the players one step forward.

Mohamed Aadroun, teacher business administration Amsterdam University of Applied Sciences

CRITICAL SUCCESS FACTOR 7

Insight into the competences of all personnel in relation to competences relevant to the organization.

Many organizations work on talent and competence management in order to develop and utilize the available talents to the extent possible. This has an important relationship with D&I because D&I, with its special balance of uniqueness and belonging, wants to engage different talents for the core activities of the organization. Talent management is not automatically adjusted to D&I. In a diverse environment, an inclusive perspective is a precondition for the observation and assessment of competences. How that works is also shown under the success factors 2, 5, 6, 8 and 10. Besides this inclusive perspective, attention is needed for the elaboration of the various competences. In examples given for behavior, D&I does not seem to play a role. Nevertheless, employees who are excellent communicators can be lost for words when they see themselves confronted with new types of interlocutors and completely miss the point.

When forms of talent or competence management are used, it influences quite a lot of systems in the organization. Therefore, it is important to integrate D&I: from job descriptions to assessments and from e-learning programs to career development (see also factor 8).

Group Competences and Individual Competences

The question arises regularly whether representatives of specific social groups do bring specific talents. Are the Dutch and the Turks better merchants than the Americans or the French? Do women have more empathy than men by nature? Are gay men more apt to work in health care than heterosexual men? This way of thinking finds its origin in the desire to get a grip on the diverse reality and to think in clearly distinguished dualities (see p. 49). Usually, the path to determine competences is more complicated. For example, it is obvious that Chinese salesmen are doing well for diamond merchants in Amsterdam and Antwerp who have a lot of Chinese customers but it is not obvious that every Chinese candidate who applies for the job will be a good salesman: other selection criteria are needed to determine that!

The starting point is that people have individual competences and no 'group competences' deriving from their background in a specific social group. Nevertheless, the general assumption is that certain 'groups' are better at something than others, so how do you consider that? Here are two examples to stimulate your line of thought:

> *There is a greater chance to find intercultural skills with people from an ethnic minority background because they already live in an intercultural situation every day. However, you can't be sure. Moreover, it doesn't mean that they do realize it themselves and that they can use it methodically for the job: that takes more. On the other side, people with a majority background can have great intercultural skills. Usually they have acquired them by working abroad or in intercultural organizations.*

The atmosphere in management teams often changes when women become part of the team. This is not because women are different as managers, but because different dynamics occur in the team as we have described under success factor 6. The same goes for other forms of mixed management teams, for example, when the first black person or an otherwise different social type becomes part of the team. Members of the existing team show different behavior, new forms of communication are developed, and new ideas are discussed. This can work out well, but an improvement is not self-evident.

These two examples show that the simple fact of belonging to a social group does not imply certain characteristics or skills. Nevertheless, increasing the amount of social types can bring advantages to the organization, particularly when D&I are deliberately managed.

Team Competences

As said, the (supposed) group competences of individual candidates who belong to a certain social group bring, only in exceptional cases, added value for your organization. Yet, following the road of competence management does actually contribute to the promise that diversity in teams generates more creativity, innovation and improved quality of decision making. A good balance between individual competences and the competences of the team as a whole is crucial for that.

> There is not enough diversity among policemen in the street. Often you see two younger policemen instead of a younger and an older policeman. That goes unnecessarily wrong, it escalates and cannot be de-escalated due to a lack of experience. This is also why people think they are discriminated against when it is a white officer while the same thing happens with black officers.
>
> Nowadays the emphasis lies more on enforcement where previously there was more emphasis on assistance. Think for example of a tramp who is asking for a light to tourists. Officers sent him away; the tramp calls them 'assholes' and then he gets a fine for insulting. Such a quick reaction undermines authority as if their good reputation has been damaged. They could also say: 'well Jack, you are drunk again' and act in line with that. But those young policemen assume that they are building authority. Thereupon the tramp throws away the fine and he gets another one for committing an environmental offense. That is another 90 euro that he will never pay so he will end up in jail. An older officer next to a young one can prevent this kind of escalations and strengthen the authority of the police.
>
> Willem Korthals Altes, senior judge Court of Amsterdam and chair complaints committee National Police

An example not to be followed is the analysis of the individual competences of a project team that has to come up with new building projects regularly and bring them from idea to plan to the go/no-go phase. All team members need to dispose of eight competences. They were assessed to them and it appears that each of them has a good result for four competences, an average result for one or two and a weak result for the rest of them. Now they all have to follow courses to bring the competences with an average or weak result to a better level. What does this mean in practice?

- The implicit starting-point of this method is uniformity; everybody is supposed to have about the same result on all eight competences.

- The value of the team is defined by the sum of the individual values; the team is an accumulation of independent individuals.

- Employees usually like to do what they are good at; in this case the organization asks them to invest a lot in things they are not good at, so their motivation drops.

However diverse the members of this team might be, it offers little added value to the organization because the organization expects the same from every team member.

Competences

Uniform qualities | Diverse qualities

Improve weaknesses | Utilize strengths

Team as a sum
3+3+3=9 | Team as a multiplication
3x3x3=27

Average performance | Outstanding performance

We can turn this example into a best practice where the added value of diversity becomes obvious. In the project team, the employees were assessed to the eight competences and the findings were identical: on four competences, the results are good, some are average and the rest is weak. The organization has defined that the team as a whole must be strong in certain competences. As a next step, the organization studies the results at the level of the team for the team as a whole.. What appears is that most team members are strong in three competences: for example, to develop and to communicate. Then there are three competences where the results differ: for example, to cooperate. However, two competences can hardly be found in the team: for example, to round off. That corresponds with the daily practice of the team. They are quite successful in starting up projects, but the archives are a mess and the time that is lost to search in systems is a real loss-maker. Yet, when a new team member has to be appointed, the selection committee is inclined to appreciate the competences that are already most common in the team like development and communication.

From the point of view of D&I, the basic consideration is that the organization utilizes especially the strong sides of each team member. Sometimes, an effort has to be made to improve weak sides, but real added value starts where every single team member gives his or her best qualities for the team as a whole. This means that the lacking competences are not to be improved by courses or training; the aspiration is rather to compose the team in such a way that all eight competences needed are represented in the team. When recruiting a new team member, the selection committee will not look for person number 8 being strong in development and communication but for someone who brings something different, something new to the team that also means added value for the team like the lacking competence: to round off. The effect is that:

- An individual team member is not a copy of the other team members; the team is not characterized by uniformity.

- The value of the team is not the sum of the value of the individual members, but the multiplication of it: it is the interaction that makes this team stronger than other teams; the best qualities are continuously identified and utilized.

- Job satisfaction is high because everybody may contribute the best he or she can offer.

I am in the core team of the Amsterdam Approach Healthy Weight, a municipal program focused on children and youth. That concerns a lot of domains: prevention via schools and redesign of the city, care for children who are already overweight, a lobby towards the food industry as well as our own policies for events and permits. These various domains have to mutually reinforce each other and that offers more opportunities than we seize right now. Our team has a program manager who values diversity and inclusion in many ways.

Recently we had a talent day where we studied how all team members work related to personality, role and approach. What I like is that our program manager then points out: 'Hey, we do not have a lot of doers, what does that mean for us?' We agreed for example that we will try to work less 'from the head' and talk more often about feelings, mutual relationships and dilemmas in the core team. We think that we can realize more synergy in doing so. Now the team members are still individual outposts with each their own domain and their own team. There is only mutual coordination. But when we stop to only react on ready-made proposals and start to brainstorm together from the beginning about certain subjects, then we can mutually reinforce each other's domain and talent. That will work out positively on the whole of the Approach Healthy Weight.

Our team itself is merely diverse; we have men and women, a Caribbean Dutch team member, members of diverse sexual orientation and different ages. However, we are all highly educated. Especially this high education results in too great a distance between us and our target group: families with an unhealthy lifestyle. My Caribbean colleague knows relatively best what is happening in those families because he maintains many contacts in our focus neighbourhoods in Amsterdam.

What I want to do now in terms of methodology is working with story tellers from our target group who will tell their story themselves in our meetings. In the autumn, we will organize another meeting for about three hundred participants from all our partners, intended to inspire them, as a reality-check and to gather new information. Because even when you have a lot of knowledge, every personal story makes your picture richer and more differentiated. You learn about the living environment of your target group and you feel more specially connected to them.

Anne Hofstede, senior communication advisor Amsterdam Approach Healthy Weight

Context of Ambiguities, Uncertainties, and Paradoxes

How do you organize that your managers think in terms of inclusive teams instead of in group competences attributed to individuals? Discussions about group competences can be exhausting and often lead to 'differences of opinion' which is of course something else than the deliberate utilization of talent. My experience is that the model mentioned above of the team as a multiplication: $3 \times 3 \times 3 = 27$ is easily appealing to managers and brings them to the essence. Also, the experience that it provides little energy when others continually stress one's weaknesses can be recognized by almost everybody and motivates to do things differently.

Cloning remains a persistent phenomenon. Even when teams decide to recruit someone with additional qualities, it happens that they make their selection based on the 'connection' rather than qualities, because they 'connect' usually easier with someone who already looks like the rest of them. D&I can feel unnatural; therefore, expect a wide range of arguments when you ask why a certain appointment did not work out.

There are increasingly more self-managed teams. The popularity of the existence of managers is decreasing, and team members want to do their jobs without being 'bothered' by managers. What matters, then, is that they are capable of forming an inclusive team and to recognize, value, and utilize each other's talents. The cutting of layers of management means that you have to assign the responsibility for D&I through a clear framework and with the right tools to the teams themselves.

CRITICAL SUCCESS FACTOR 8

Consolidate D&I- principles in systems and instruments for strategic personnel policy, communication policy, marketing policy and management style.

A Dutch proverb says "it is difficult to catch hares with the help of a cow." To see results, motivation and commitment are important, but also the application of appropriate tools and systems. Organizations have many tools and systems, but when it comes to diversity, they have some blind spots. My experience is that organizations hardly realise yet that they are trying to catch hares with the help of a cow. It is unavoidable to make the effort of a good analysis of tools and systems, starting with the ones that are used most.

Consolidation of D&I principles is a factor that can well be realized and measured. That is an advantage compared to other critical success factors in this book like commitment, organizational culture or added value for customers that seem to be less 'tangible.' The consolidation of D&I principles offers something visible to hang on to, especially for people who have little insight yet in what D&I implies. Thus, the implementation of D&I becomes less a stroke of luck and more a targeted policy for them. Consolidation offers practical guidelines and makes things go more automatically.

They will certainly see results when they do. You will not only catch more hares but also rabbits, foxes and even ermines will come your way as for this success factor the efforts might be big but the rewards are often and unexpectedly triple!

The examples of physical conditions, personnel policies, communication and management style show you from different angles how to apply or adjust tools and systems in the light of D&I. That information helps you to have a critical look at the tools and systems in your own organization in D&I respect.

Physical Conditions

You have invited a promising candidate for an interview. It concerns a woman with a technological background, a combination that is not very common and that you would like to have in your organization. Moreover, she has a lot of experience with large projects. Your interview committee of three is waiting for her arrival when you receive a call. The candidate will be late because she stands at the entrance but your building is not accessible for wheelchairs. You suddenly realize that the interview room isn't either.

There are different kinds of physical disabilities and solutions. For a long time, technological solutions allow blind and partially sighted employees to work with computers that read their email aloud for them and so on. But an organization must be willing to install the technique; in many countries, subsidies can be given so that money is not a problem. Still some companies think it is 'too much trouble' to do so. Also, the employees must be willing to consider the disabilities of a colleague. Recently, a blind employee described how colleagues would answer a phone call and take a message for him, often putting a yellow post-it card with the message written on it on his computer screen. That way, some messages never got to him, although the alternative is simple enough: put the message in an email, so that the computer reads it aloud when he returns at his desk. A similar example was given by a judge in a court who was hard of hearing. He is quite good at lip-speech reading, but in a court session he is dependent of a room with extra facilities. The court indeed has several rooms like that, but the planners changed sessions, and that is how he repeatedly ends up in rooms without facilities. Consequently, he has to stand up for himself and keep on reminding the others that he has a disability.

The cooperation of colleagues is vital, even when technical solutions have been installed. Nevertheless, for employees with a disability, the physical conditions in the organization form the starting point for the utilization of their talents. If a candidate in a wheelchair cannot even enter the building of your organization, the party ends before it even started.

Tools for Personnel Policy

It re-occurs in D&I land on a regular basis: 'anonymous recruitment,' by hiding the names of candidates who write letters of application. There is far sufficient research showing that candidates with a 'foreign' name are less often invited for job interviews than candidates with a name that is perceived as 'familiar' in background. In other words: there is discrimination in the labor market. Anonymous recruitment is supposed to bring the solution for this and like usual with this kind of issues, this approach is surrounded by a fierce discussion, both in the organization and in public debate.

Those in favor are happy to finally see the recognition that discrimination exists and that something is done about it. Adversaries consider this as a permissive instrument for discrimination that only fights the symptoms. What other characteristics will be hidden next: age? Because discrimination on the labor market also affects elderly people. They think this is a false solution.

The discussion that arises about anonymous recruitment shows the struggle to find the right tools for organizations who want to give equal opportunities to all candidates. Although the opposite has often been stated, most tests and assessments used in recruitment processes are not designed for cross-cultural use. This is not just a linguistic problem for second language candidates but also a problem of interpretation; assumptions about 'the right answer' are culturally biased as well as assumptions about what answers are indicative of what personality types. Most tests were developed in a time that the world of organizations was a lot less diverse than nowadays. Moreover, many psychologists and others who are involved in testing do not have diversity competence (see success factor 5) even when they claim they do.

For organizations who want to work with D&I-proof tools, a thorough orientation is necessary. A natural rule applies here: the more you know about it yourself, the better you can buy. Make sure that the purchasing department and the employees who deal with the development of personnel systems are knowledgeable about D&I. Also, invest in some research to find out who your organization invites or does not invite for job interviews: how inclusive are the results?

You can check all your tools and systems for personnel policy in the same way, think of:

- Texts and photographs or pictures in advertisements
- Bureaus for recruitment, training, e-systems
- E-learning systems, e-platforms
- Forms
- Flexible working hours
- Letters
- Competence management
- Job descriptions
- Evaluation procedures
- Tools and systems for career development
- Management development
- Annual plan, reviews and reports

- Training and education

- Introduction days

- Terms of employment

The heart of the matter is that all these tools and systems should foster the recognition, the utilization and the retention of diverse talents for your organization and that they are free of eventual exclusion mechanisms.

Procedures Concerning (Un)wanted Conduct

What every diverse and inclusive organization needs are procedures to handle discrimination, sexual intimidation and mobbing. The guiding principles must be very clear for everybody involved in case of complaints and unacceptable behavior. Besides clear guiding principles that can be found on paper and intranet you need a specially trained counsellor with:

- knowledge of procedures

- insight in D&I at work and (un)wanted conduct

- process skills to support the persons involved in the best possible way.

Codes of conduct form a good instrument to encourage wanted conduct. In a code of conduct, a company defines the rules of the game and the rules for good social behavior. In that sense, it is a positive instrument. It determines specifically what the organization wants. A code of conduct is a tool to talk about workplace behavior: it gives words to informal rules and direction in conduct. Some companies ask all new employees to sign the code of conduct. It is a way of showing that they value good social behavior as much as the more material conditions in the employment contract. It differs per country how a method like actually signing a code of conduct will be received, but in companies where it was applied already, experiences are usually favorable.

Instruments for Communication and Marketing

It may seem obvious: the tools and system your organization uses for communication and marketing should match your D&I policy. However, it is not automatic. Look for example at the website of companies who do not just give written information about the company, including their D&I policy, but also photographs of their board. It is still quite frequent that besides the wonderful words about the value of diversity for the organization only pictures of 'white men with grey hairs and ties' can be found on the website. What would be the effect on visitors of the site? And what if they start blogging about it and publish that for anyone to read? For example, recently a famous journalist blogged after her experience when signing up for a course of Weight Watchers via their site:

> *These are the images Weight Watchers uses to appeal to their target group: all white, slim women in the age of thirty with straight, long hair. You can call me oversensitive but if this represents the Weight Watchers-customer, what should I do there, as a fat, almost-fifty-year-old woman with short hair?[9]*

This of course is not the PR Weight Watchers would like to have; certainly, there are a lot of people older than thirty years with short hair in their target group. If your organization values D&I, all tools and systems for communication and marketing have to be considered and evaluated. Promotional gifts, Christmas presents, your personnel magazine, intranet, internet, end-of-year reports: the message will only come across when it is consistent.

The increasingly diverse society makes it difficult to predict who will be reached by what message. There are numerous media both online and offline. Recruitment policies are usually adjusted at an early stage but the policies for information and advice to customers often form a challenge. The average letter of official authorities is difficult to read and rarely uses visual material. Participation meetings often show a public that is not diverse in terms of social types and level of education even when cities are. Policy makers blame the disinterest of citizens for that. Also, commercial companies could have much better communication results when they take into account the diversity of the public.

For example, the collection agency Syncasso discovered that the use of images in letters, already upon the envelope, improves the response of people with debts drastically and their perception of the engagement of the bailiff is more positive. Not everyone dares to open an envelope just like that, especially not when in big trouble, and not everyone is a written-text-enthusiast. Communication that aims at a certain effect in a diverse environment requires knowledge of the diverse customers and their way to absorb a message. A varying, instead of uniform, tone of voice is also part of the Syncasso approach; dependent of the stage of the payment process the customer is in more kind in the beginning, more pressing when a court case is imminent. As changes in the world, the people, the habits and the lifestyles accelerate, the effect of existing tools and systems for communication and marketing cannot be predicted beforehand. Therefore, Syncasso developed the new communication methods not just on their own but in cooperation with scientific researchers. D&I did not just fall into their lap. Indeed, the investments in D&I led to measurable better results.

More and more companies and institutions experiment with new tools where communication and marketing are rather two-sided, both sending and receiving: forms of dialogue, (digital) participation instruments, panels, and debates. A company

---

[9] http://www.karinameerman.nl/weightwatchers/

can advertise but it can also organize an activity with a certain social group that has possible attractive job candidates for the company or specific customers. Thus, the targeted social groups get more familiar with the organization and they are more likely to be appreciated as future employer or service provider. In the meantime, the organization learns more about the diverse lifestyles and wishes and can respond more appropriately to them.

Whatever choices your organization makes, it has of course to be consistent with your business case for D&I (see success factor 1). Avoid, however, the thought that employees work with ill-considered assumptions and make assessment faults when they speak to the press, hoping that the journalist will just understand why they write Happy Spring instead of Happy Easter in the new leaflet. The possible consequence is that it might not be the tool your organization uses that is expensive, but the research that your organization has to do to use the tool in the right way. In the light of D&I, reflections on the right way deserve your attention also.

Management Style

Not every organization is consciously choosing and creating a certain management style. Quite often, it is a style that has somehow developed 'automatically.' In that case it is difficult to call the management style a tool. Nevertheless, it is very well possible to turn the management style into a tool that works for D&I in the organization. Most suitable is the coaching, inspiring style. In the increasingly diverse world, managers depend more on the initiatives of entrepreneurial and inclusive thinking employees who see and seize opportunities, rather than on people who do what they are told to do within the span of control the managers can handle. This is in line with the more general trend of 'less management, more facilitation' and the creation of self-directed teams where the managers' first task is to create the condition for the employees to achieve the best performance. Guiding seems to be more indirect in that case but it still enables working on D&I. A manager studies, for example, what the barriers are for the personal responsibility of employees and continues to highlight the vision of D&I; he or she confronts employees with best practices and brings the diverse outside world of customers into the organization; he or she stimulates the employees to acquire more skills related to inclusive teams and inclusive customer treatment.

Applying management style as a tool for D&I means that the organization has worked out clear ideas about that style, ideally together with the employees who will be confronted with that application. And just like the employees that the manager is going to manage, the managers in turn may expect from the leaders of the organization to treat them with a coaching and inspiring style even when they still find it difficult to apply the new, for D&I suitable style themselves.

Context of Ambiguities, Uncertainties, and Paradoxes

The biggest uncertainty lies in the question whether people really use the existing tools and systems in the right, intended way. Indeed, the context of uncertainty here is more inside the organization than outside. The good news is that you can influence that context more than average. Another big uncertainty lies with the tools and systems for which you use external professionals like assessments. The denial of D&I mechanisms is quite persistent in certain circles of professionals. Due to procurement constructions, you might have to continue working for a long time with some unwilling agencies.

CRITICAL SUCCESS FACTOR 9

Sufficient diversity at all levels of the organization.

Working to have sufficient diversity in the sense of recruitment and internal advancement for a specific social group evokes more emotions and commotion than almost any other issue when implementing D&I in organizations. Paradoxically, it is, in the meantime, the success factor that most companies have already tried to implement or that they are actually working on. You'll notice when you speak about D&I in the organization: the first connection employees make is 'positive action for women and minorities' and that is not always positive. Still also this success factor is necessary.

> To what extent does the outside world have an affinity with jurisdiction and do they recognize it? In criminal cases, the vast majority has a black or migrant background. Rarely there is a judge with the same background. We are a part of society but we do not reflect it. We are seen as people from the dominant white Dutch society. With the best will in the world judges try to communicate with very diverse people and they are trained to do so. Nevertheless, the affiliation is still very limited.
>
> Willem Korthals Altes, senior judge Court of Amsterdam and chair complaints committee National Police.

Especially, for more women in leadership positions, there is increasing pressure in society; I wrote in the introduction about leading investors and under success factor 2 about the introduction of rules and laws by governments because of the vision that companies thrive with diverse teams at the top. Although the Netherlands are a very free country that values equality, they are no forerunner here, as many people assume. They rather rank bottom in Europe, both for women in Executive and Non-Executive Boards and on universities, where the number of female professors also lags behind (now 18 percent). It makes no difference whether it is about healthcare, with many female employees, or in technology, where the number of female employees, is low in the Netherlands: the percentages of women at the top are similar. Therefore, the issue of positive action for women stays on the agenda. But in the meantime, there is a huge need to widen the scope of D&I activities. After all, a human being is more than just a man or woman; internationalization and multidisciplinary working ways lead to new urgencies.

There is no such thing as the ultimate, conclusive solution to work on sufficient diversity in numbers of social types. Each solution has its own downside. Therefore, well-considered choices are needed to make everybody understand what solution suits best for this particular organization, based on a well-formulated business case with vision on diversity and what the results for the organization should be. Differences are more than just the visible aspects, think of the teams who invent the applications for Smart Cities: besides technical staff also a behavioral specialist, a communication specialist and a management scientist might bring added value to the team as well as staff who understand how diverse social groups, like the elderly or people in socially deprived areas, deal with new applications.

> Because of the last-in, first-out principle at budget cuts, a lot of diversity disappears, also in our institution. There are now two ways to go, one is to let go of the last in first out principle. Indeed, diversity is an important wish of our clients. The other way is to look for cooperation with interest- and grassroots organizations to meet with the client wishes.
>
> Fawzia Nasrullah, CEO youthcare institution Youké

10 Ways to Work on Sufficient Diversity at All Levels of the Organization

1. Positive Discrimination

Positive discrimination means that an organization reserves certain vacancies for one or more specifically designated social groups, for example women, Afro-Americans, or people with a disability. Whoever have no characteristics that match with people from these groups are excluded from the selection procedure. Such a measure can be experienced as very unfair by those who are a different social group.

The most important advantage of positive discrimination is that your organization has short term results in attracting staff from more diverse backgrounds. As said this can evoke a lot of resistance. Obviously, positive discrimination only considers certain specific differences between people, thus amplifying rather than reducing the perception of visible differences. It can make us forget about the larger and deeper diversity in human beings that we cannot observe; then it will be overlooked instead of utilized and inclusion is just far away.

Another important disadvantage of positive discrimination is that it augments the internal orientation of your organization. Although the opportunities of D&I lie in the communication with the world outside, organizations often spend their time in internal fights about the personnel policy proposed. In doing so, the diverse customer is usually forgotten and the sensitivity for external signals rather becomes less than more.

2. Priority Policy

A lighter form of positive discrimination is priority policy or positive action. This policy allows everybody to apply for the job, but in the case of 'equal ability' or 'equal quality' a candidate from the designated social groups gets the priority. Priority policy has the same advantages and disadvantages as positive discrimination.

Specifically, with priority policy, comes the long-lasting discussion about 'ability' and 'quality,' since equal ability or equal quality do not exist. It leads to a lot of discussion during recruitment processes. Research for scientific appointment has shown that as a matter of fact in the last round there are no comparable differences any more between the remaining candidates. At that point, the context and the group process are decisive. How do members of the selection committee present candidates, does anyone support a specific candidate? In the decisive last round, criteria have become factually ambiguous and then it all ends up to perceptions and networks.

3. Find New Channels and Networks for Recruitment

Many organizations achieved good results in finding new channels for recruitment. When you have defined a business case that needs the recruitment of more people from different social types, dare to broaden the perspectives, to explore new (offline and online) networks. Make new connections and work with different tools. It may sound logical, but all too often, also because of their workload, recruiters hang on to their usual routine; breaking routines is possible but requires an effort.

4. Diverse Interview Committees

Essential is the diversity within the interview committee itself. Organizations better compose their committees with a team of different social types. The assumption for that, which is supported by a lot of research, is that a diverse committee will not so easily reject different types of candidates. A committee with men only is inclined to prefer a male candidate; a committee with white people only is inclined to underestimate the qualities of a candidate of color.

5. Training of Interview Committees

Another useful method is training interview committees. In this training, the committee members learn to deal with different (D&I) perspectives in relation to diverse candidates when making their choice. A method related to this is training-on-the-job, where a D&I expert joins the team in the different steps of the selection process, asks questions, gives feedback and works with them in practice to make the assessment of the committee members D&I-friendly.

6. Culture-based Recruitment

Organizations are more and more able to assess whether candidates are fit for a function (job fit) but this still hardly goes for the match with the organizational culture (cultural fit). An international survey in 54 countries, among which 63 percent was in Europe, revealed that employers generally recognize the value of a good match with the organizational culture (cultural fit), they even consider it as almost as important as job fit. However, in many cases there is no description of the organizational culture yet, neither have methods been developed to measure the cultural fit. Still candidates are regularly rejected based on a lack of cultural fit.

From the perspective of D&I, I see culture-based recruitment as an opportunity because in all social types candidates can be found who are culturally fit. That way, the utilization and retention of diverse talents can run more smoothly and successfully. However, without clear cultural criteria the social types that are 'different' will be the first to be confronted with rejection. Culture-based recruitment thus forms an exciting new path that deserves a chance also for D&I.

7. Recruitment based on Team Analysis

A quite different approach that is also effective takes the needs of the team as a starting-point. The profile of the candidate to be appointed is worked out based on an analysis of the team he or she will join. What background, education or experience will offer added value? This approach reflects ideas as elaborated under critical success factor 7. By the way, the famous football expert Johan Cruyff already told us years ago when talking about the recruitment of the best talents for football teams: 'Quality comes first, but quality always has to serve the team as a whole.'

8. Targets for Managers

By making targets part of the management contracts of your managers, clear agreements can be made. Your managers feel more responsible for D&I in appointments when they have explicitly agreed to the targets. Nevertheless, resistance is to be expected and will need your attention. Besides you have to be aware of the nature of the targets: make retention a part of them as well as recruitment and promotion. Otherwise, it is possible that new appointments are realized, but the total figures of diversity don't improve because the front door of your company is wide open, but so is the back door.

9. Internal Network Development

Network development supports the career advancement of more different social types in your organization. Some organizations form networks for especially designated social types: a women's network, a network for people of color, a gay and lesbian network, a network of high potentials and so on. Others have a broader view of D&I and start a network where everybody who wants to help building organizational innovation can join. In practice, these networks have an excellent role in breaking through existing routines in work methods, assessment and promotion. They make traditional routines visible and support their members to find their way through the organization. They offer role models and increase the likelihood of retention of diverse employees. Network members stimulate each other to respond to vacancies and actively work on career advancement. Keep in mind that experience shows these networks need a sponsor in the top of your organization for the best effect.

10. Mentoring

A popular method to improve personnel retention is mentoring. Mentors support new employees during the first months in the organization. Thus, new employees can feel that they belong and they find their way through the organization more easily. Mentoring systems can also be applied with a view to climbing the ladder. Managers in higher levels of the organization serve as a mentor and/or role model for employees who are considered as high-potentials, who follow a MD-course, who are members of female or migrant or gay networks and so on. The experiences with mentoring systems are almost invariably successful.

Context of Ambiguities, Uncertainties, and Paradoxes

This factor is absolutely surrounded with ambiguities, uncertainties and paradoxes as you can read in the description of the various methods above. Moreover, many organizations already have experience with this success factor and that created particular perceptions about it, as well within your organization as in the environment. Whatever you want to set in motion for this factor, make sure you have a well-considered track and ingenious communication to prevent that opponents hurry to discredit your plans. In an unexpected moment, press and politics can also start to interfere; your good preparation is an important prerequisite for effective responses.

A specific uncertainty lies in the domain of ethnic-religious background. For example, during many years, it was forbidden for Dutch people with Iranian roots to fulfill certain functions, particularly in nuclear disciplines. Brilliant people saw their ambitions frustrated to contribute to the field and our society. In the meantime, the Netherlands was the country where one of the most important nuclear spies (with Pakistani background) acquired information of inestimable value; therefore, such a measure could meet with quite some consensus, despite the individual tragic consequences it brought.

Actuality brings us a variety of new 'enemies.' Will actual measures look like the old ones, when communists were not at all welcome in the Dutch army? Does the nature of generic measures match with the actual age of increasing diversity? These questions do not just occur for security services or high-end ICT and weapon development, but also in the more traditional economy because economy is also a form of war and in a worldwide economy espionage and the risk of hostile takeovers or erosion from within are the new reality. This cannot be solved just like that. It requires your keen attention. Be sure that acting based on vision and self-confidence always wins from uncertainty and defensive behavior. If you doubt about the dilemmas here, then just face that and work on them with the best advisers you can find in this domain.

CRITICAL SUCCESS FACTOR 10

Board and management are evaluated on the basis of actions and behavior concerning D&I

There are few best practices to be found in organizations when looking for inspiration on evaluation on the basis of actions and behavior concerning D&I. Even when there is a certain commitment to D&I in an organization, managers find it hard to accept that they would be evaluated in this respect. And organizations usually facilitate managers for an easy way out. Indeed, several conditions are needed to make evaluation possible:

a. Clear targets

If targets can be found at all, they usually concern the recruitment and promotion of a certain social type of employees (see success factor 9). Targets with respect to actions and behavior are rare, think for example of:

- improving customer satisfaction at the counter

- improving employee satisfaction or team satisfaction

- a higher percentage of customers among diverse ethnic shopkeepers or female entrepreneurs

- increasing use of certain services or products by specific customer groups

- innovation in services offered or in the adoption of applications by various social groups

b. Competences for managers

Competences are still considered as a diversity neutral issue. Cooperation, communication, leadership, non-of these competences seems to be influenced by the context managers work in: uniform or diverse. This has been elaborated already under the success factors 5, 6 and 7. When an issue is not a part of the competences that come with a function, evaluating it is, of course, quite complicated, both at the first appointment of new managers and at assessments and eventual promotion.

c. Management development

Knowledge or skills that managers don't have yet when they enter the organization can indeed be a part of the management development program. However, D&I is hardly covered in those programs yet. Companies do have specific workshops for D&I that are somehow separate or part of a temporary project. Organizations start to realize that D&I is a quality manager should master, but yet they hardly integrate it into the regular management development program. Thus, it cannot be part of the regular systems for assessment and evaluation either.

d. The natural inclination to produce clones

An evaluation is never completely objective and we shouldn't pretend that it can be so. What matters is to have a good self-knowledge about one's own perceptions and the ever-present inclination to gather clones around us. This inclination impedes a good inclusive assessment and remuneration in the organization. Cloning is related to the token theory as described under success factor 2 and comes with a certain amount of self-confidence and dedication: most managers are positive about their own contribution and work so when they have to appoint a successor or a colleague they prefer a person that looks like themselves as much as possible. They are convinced to serve the organization in the right way. The challenge is not to ban the phenomenon of cloning but to know that it exists and to act with full awareness about it. I have already elaborated on the necessary insights and skills to do this under the success factors 5 and 6. Without these, a good evaluation based on actions and behavior concerning D&I is impossible.

A good evaluation of D&I practices requires certain conditions in the organization that are hardly met with until now. Thus, we get caught in a vicious circle where D&I can only be implemented when it is part of the evaluation of managers but where the conditions for this evaluation are not being met yet by lack of implementation. All too often, D&I is considered as an idealistic issue, good for socially engaged managers or managers who believe in corporate social responsibility: D&I as a toy for managers who like it. If they don't, that doesn't influence their evaluation.

> You become an inclusive leader when you do your work with passion: it's that simple! Once you have tasted the richness of the international, you understand more. The corporate philosophy should be that the company performs better as the leadership becomes more inclusive. However, when there is nothing to suggest that the role and activities of the inclusive leader are recognized and valued, it is not going to work.
>
> Marij Urlings, director Domain Education & Innovation, Inholland University of Applied Sciences

Context of Ambiguities, Uncertainties, and Paradoxes

As inclusive leader, you break with old routines and shift the evaluation from (supposed) idealism to actions for the benefit of the organization. Like for success factor 8, your context lies more inside than outside the organization; therefore, you can influence it quite well. Make sure your managers can score with D&I and let them do it so that real results are achieved:

- Make sure the evaluation is based on a good business case for D&I.

- Use methods that have already proven their success for other domains in your organization. Build on experience, what makes your managers move?

- Don't do everything at the same time. Start where you can and develop step by step a more complete evaluation system.

- Also include hard-to-measure ('soft') elements in the evaluation.

- Do not just apply the evaluation and comparability at individual level but also use it for discussion among your managers.

- Show public appreciation. Publicize the good actions of your managers, show best practices, share your recognition or hand out awards. Despite humbling and grumbling in the corridors, telling that an award is nonsense and 'means nothing,' those who receive public recognition are truly proud and happy with the publicity that comes with it; and others around them are more prepared to go the extra mile.

Organizing: The Last, but not the Least, Aspect of Inclusive Leadership

Besides giving direction and exemplary behavior, organizing is the important third aspect of the model for Inclusive Leadership, even when it is not always the favorite aspect of leaders because of the risk that lies in the many details of organizing. Practice has shown that the interference of leaders themselves is still essential, on the one side because there is little knowledge about and experience with D&I, on the other side because many initiatives concerning D&I run aground for lack of time, attention and facilitation from the top.

The methodology of 10 critical success factors allows you to introduce D&I as a business issue in your organization and to apply D&I as integral part of your core business. It gives a framework and a terminology that facilitates the dialogue between all different departments. It allows for exchange about the perception of chances and the weighting of priorities. The methodology is about how and not about what and supports you to define what proceeds of D&I you want for your organization.

There are sufficient enthusiast people and successful methods to make it work. You, as a leader, have deeply reflected about the strategy, you determine what will or will not work for your organization and you facilitate the people who address the issues that call for operational action. This is how giving direction, showing exemplary behavior, and organizing mutually reinforce each other so that even in a context of uncertainties, dilemmas and paradoxes you utilize the advantages of diversity in your inclusive organization.

Epilogue

The starting point of this book was a casual question I asked to a colleague in my field when the subject of Inclusive Leadership emerged: 'What exactly is that?' Despite my in-depth questions, I got little more explanation than that inclusive leadership is about the exemplary behavior of the leader. That disappointed me: should we not expect more from leaders than just exemplary behavior? In fact, a lot more is needed than just behavior. Further research showed me that the term inclusive leadership is mentioned regularly but that as a concept it has hardly been filled in with 'content.' So inevitably, a new book was born.

Beyond the Difference is the result of literature studies, experience in practice and the valuable contributions of a number of leaders who have been active during years in the field of diversity & inclusion. In this book, quotes can be read from interviews with:

- Mohamed Aadroun, teacher business administration Amsterdam University of Applied Sciences

- Atilla Aytekin, CEO of Orange Games

- Anne Hofstede, senior communication advisor Amsterdam Approach Healthy Weight

- Willem Korthals Altes, senior judge Court of Amsterdam and chair complaints committee National Police

- Fawzia Nasrullah, CEO of youthcare institution Youké

- André Peperkoorn, deputy commander Royal Netherlands Marechaussee.

- Marij Urlings, director Domain Education & Innovation, Inholland University of Applied Sciences

I owe special gratitude to Marij Urlings and Anne Hofstede for their lecture and comments of texts and concepts. The support of professor John Grin was brilliant, both in the conceptualisation and in the structuring of this book, for which I thank him. Our dialogue will certainly continue during many years to come. I am the only one to blame for eventual shortcomings of this book.

It is my conviction and also my concern that we have difficult years ahead for diversity and inclusion, inside organizations as well as in the world outside. In the meantime, it is exactly in a smart and targeted approach of D&I that opportunities occur for organizations who think across silos and borders and who are strong in trade, customer relations, and innovation. Inclusive leadership is of inestimable value for prosperity, both materially and immaterially. With this book, I wish to shed light for you on the fascinating actual context of ambiguity, uncertainty and paradoxes and offer you a clear framework for your reflections and actions. Your reaction is more than welcome at g.vangeffen@seba.nl.

BIBLIOGRAPHY

van Arensbergen, P., P. van den Besselaar, and I. van der Weijden. (2014). 'The selection of talent as a group process.' *A literature review on the social dynamics of decision making in grant panels.* Oxford University Press.

van Arensbergen, P., *Talent Proof: Selection processes in research funding and careers,* Dissertation Rathenau Instituut 2014.

Belinski, E., K. Hansen & Ursula Müller (Hg.), *Diversity Management: Best Practices im internationalen Feld,* Bd. 2, Lit Verlag, Münster 2003.

Bijsterveldt, M. van (eindred.), 'Receptenboek homoseksualiteit in het onderwijs,' *uitgave COC Nederland,* Amsterdam 2005.

Brewer, M. B., S. Otten & K. van der Zee, *Towards inclusive organizations determinants of successful diversity management at work,* Psychology Press London 2015.

Bruine, A.M. de, 'Valid Express; waar mensen met lastige lichamen tot ontplooiing komen,' *Uitgeverij SWP,* Amsterdam 2003.

Cubiks, *International Survey on Job and Cultural Fit,* 2013

Geffen, G. H. van, 'De interculturele delen TaalAnker reeks,' *Uitgeverij Kluwer,* Alphen aan den Rijn:

9) Interculturele Communicatie, 2001

13) Intercultureel Samenwerken, 2001

17) Etnomarketing, verkopen aan allochtone Nederlanders, 2002

20) Omgaan met Cultuurverschillen, 2002

23) Intercultureel zakendoen, 2002

30) Interculturele problemen op de werkvloer, 2002

35) Interculturele omgangsvormen, 2003

———, *Resultaten van de 5th en 6th International Diversity Conference in Beijing* 2005 en New Orleans in 2006, Seba Amsterdam.

———, 'Making the Difference, Common Ground Publishing LLC 2010

———, *Werving en selectie: waar een wil is zonder weg, op.* www.managementsite.nl 2010.

———, *Intercultureel samenwerken op www.managementsite.nl,* 2010.

———, 'Diversity op de werkvloer,' *uitgeverij Kluwer,* boek oktober 2011.

———, 'Simpel is het moeilijkst,' in *HO management vakblad voor management en bestuur van HBO en WO-instellingen,* Sdu Uitgevers, September 2012.

————, 'Kwaliteit staat op nummer één,' *over diversity in de governance van woningcorporaties*, uitgeverij Diversity Shop, 2012.

Handschuck, 'S.Grundlagen interkultureller Kompetenz für Jobcenter und Arbeitsagenturen,' *IQ Fachstelle VIA Bayern*, 2015.

Hateley, B., & W. Schmidt, 'A peacock in the land of penguins a tale of diversity and discover,' *Berrett-Koehler Publishers*, San Francisco 1997.

Hofstede, G., 'Cultures and organizations software of the mind,' *HarperCollinsBusiness,* London 1991.

Hofstede, G. J., P. B. Petersen & G. Hofstede, 'Werken met cultuurverschillen,' *Business Contact*, Amsterdam 2006.

Hofstede, M., 'Ontkiemend zaad,' *Stichting IVIO*, Lelystad 1998.

Jackson, S. E., A. Joshi & N. L. Erhard, 'Recent Research on Team and Organizational Diversity: SWOT Analysis and Implications,' *Journal of Management,* Volume 29, Issue 6, December 2003, Pages 801-830.

Kanter, Rosabeth Moss, 'Men and Women of the Corporation,' *Basic Books* New York.

Kim, S. S. & M. J. Gelfand, 'The influence of ethnic identity on perceptions of organizational recruitment,' *Journal of Vocational Behavior,* Volume 63, Issue 3, December 2003, Pages 396-416.

Koall, I., V. Bruchhagen & F. Höher (Hg.), 'Vielfalt statt Lei(d)tkultur,' *Managing Gender & Diversity*, Lit Verlag, Münster 2002.

————, *Diversity Outlooks, Managing diversity zwischen Ethik, Profit und Antidiskriminierung*, Lit Verlag, Hamburg 2007.

Raaijmakers, M., *Authentiek verbinden*, Rijksuniversiteit Groningen 2008.

Roosevelt Thomas, Jr., R., 'Building a house for diversity,' *Amacom*, New York 1999.

Shadid, W. A., 'Grondslagen van de interculturele communicatie,' *Kluwer*, Alphen aan den Rijn 1997.

Shore, L. M., A. E. Randel, B. G. Chung, M. A. Dean, K. Holcombe Ehrhart & G. Singh, 'Inclusion and Diversity in Work Groups: A Review and Model for Future Research,' *Journal of Management* 2011 37: 1262 originally published online 28 October 2010.

Smelik, A. e.a., Effectief beeldvormen theorie, 'analyze en praktijk van beeldvormingsprocessen,' *Van Gorcum*, Assen 1999.

Turning diversity into prosperity; 'kansen voor wie investeert in diversity,' *uitgave van Companies van Companies for Diversity* 2007 (Seba Amsterdam).

Turning Diversity into Prosperity, 'Best Practices book,' *uitgave met best van Companies for Diversity*, juni 2009.

Ven, van der C., 'Zeggen wat onzichtbaar is,' *FC Klap*, Hilversum 2003. Wie bindt, 'die wint; war for talent,' *Trendboek Content* 2006.

Websites (in Jan/Feb 2016):

http://joshbersin.com/2015/12/why-diversity-and-inclusion-will-be-a-top-priority-for-
2016/

http://nl.sodexo.com/files/live/sites/sdxcom-nl/files/050C_Country.com
Netherlands(Dutch)/Building_Blocks/LOCAL/Multimedia/PDF/2014/Sod
exo_duurzaamheids_factsheet_boekjaar_2013_7_definitief.pdf

https://www.universiteitleiden.nl/en/dossiers/diversity/our-vision-of-diversity

http://www.validexpress.nl/content/werken-bij-valid-express

https://www.pwc.com/gx/en/about/diversity.html

https://actueel.pwc.nl/diensten-en-sectoren/corporate-governance/commissarissen-als-
bewakers-van-cultuur-en-gedrag/

http://ombud.mit.edu/sites/default/files/documents/micro-affirm-ineq.pdf

http://www.karinameerman.nl/weightwatchers/

http://uk.businessinsider.com/blackrock-ceo-larry-fink-letter-to-sp-500-ceos-2016-
2?r=US&IR=T

http://www.grantthornton.cn/en/Presspercent20room/2015/News1446101672327.html

http://www.zipconomy.nl/2016/02/pwc-lanceert-talent-exchange-matcht-interim-
talent-met-projecten/

http://www2.deloitte.com/content/dam/Deloitte/nl/Documents/public-sector/deloitte-
nl-ps-smart-cities-report.pdf

http://www.asito.nl/Over-ons/Kracht-van-Kleur.aspx

https://www.unilever.nl/news/overig-nieuws/2014/unilever-streeft-naar-diversity.html

Beyond the Difference

About the Author

Grethe van Geffen works as an expert in culture, diversity and inclusion since 1997 with her company Seba cultuurmanagement. She has experience in almost all sectors as consultant, trainer and project manager and knows what is at stake at different levels of the organizations. She has given many presentations, trainings and workshops inside and outside her homeland the Netherlands (including Belgium, China, Denmark, Germany, France, Jordan, Malawi, Morocco, Tunisia and the USA). Her publication list contains 13 books and over 30 articles in the field of D&I. Moreover, she publishes materials and methods under the label Diversity Shop and Diversity Video in order to support the quality of training and consultancy work in professionals' practices.

Grethe is active in board committees such as the Dutch Mensa Foundation and the Amsterdam Andalusian Orchestra. Before that she was, among others, on the board of the Chamber of Commerce Amsterdam and Urban Youthwork Amsterdam. She also chaired the members' organization of Mensa the Netherlands and the Emancipation Advisory Council Amsterdam.

She speaks Dutch, German, English, French, Turkish and some Spanish.

http://nl.linkedin.com/in/grethevangeffen
www.seba.nl
www.diversityshop.nl
www.diversityvideo.eu